DO WE NEED RELIGION?

THE YALE CULTURAL SOCIOLOGY SERIES

Jeffrey C. Alexander and Ron Eyerman, Series Editors

PUBLISHED

Triumph and Trauma, by Bernhard Giesen (2004)

Myth, Meaning, and Performance: Toward a New Cultural Sociology of the Arts, edited by Ron Eyerman and Lisa McCormick (2006)

American Society: A Theory of Societal Community, by Talcott Parsons, edited and introduced by Giuseppe Sciortino (2007)

The Easternization of the West: A Thematic Account of Cultural Change in the Modern Era, by Colin Campbell (2007)

Culture, Society, and Democracy: The Interpretive Approach, edited by Isaac Reed and Jeffrey C. Alexander (2007)

Changing Men, Transforming Culture: Inside the Men's Movement, by Eric Magnuson (2007)

Do We Need Religion? On the Experience of Self-Transcendence, by Hans Joas (2008)

An Introduction to Contemporary Sociology: Culture and Society in Transition, by Jeffrey C. Alexander and Kenneth Thompson (2008)

FORTHCOMING

Émile Durkheim Today, by Mustafa Emirbayer

Making Los Angeles: How People Create Place Out of Ordinary Urban Space, by Christopher D. Campbell

Jihadi Terrorism in the Modern World, by Farhad Khosrokhavar

Staging Solidarity: Truth and Reconciliation in the New South Africa, by Tanya Goodman

Meaning and Method: The Cultural Approach to Sociology, edited by Isaac Reed and Jeffrey C. Alexander

DO WE NEED RELIGION?

ON THE EXPERIENCE
OF SELF-TRANSCENDENCE

Hans Joas

Translated from German by Alex Skinner

Paradigm Publishers

Boulder • London

Paradigm Publishers is committed to preserving our environment. This book was printed on recycled paper with 30% post-consumer waste content, saving trees and avoiding the creation of hundreds of gallons of wastewater, tens of pounds of solid waste, more than a hundred pounds of greenhouse gases, and using hundreds fewer kilowatt hours of electricity than if it had been printed on paper manufactured from all virgin fibers.

Originally published in German as *Braucht der Mensch Religion? Über Erfahrungen der Selbsttrauszendenz* (Freiburg: Herder, 2003). German edition © 2003 Hans Joas

Published in the United States by Paradigm Publishers, 3360 Mitchell Lane Suite E, Boulder, CO 80301 USA.

Paradigm Publishers is the trade name of Birkenkamp & Company, LLC, Dean Birkenkamp, President and Publisher.

Library of Congress Cataloging-in-Publication Data

Joas, Hans, 1948–
    Do we need religion? : on the experience of self-transcendence / by Hans Joas.
    p. cm. — (The yale cultural sociology series)
    ISBN-13: 978-1-59451-438-8 (hardcover : alk. paper)
    ISBN-13: 978-1-59451-439-5 (pbk. : alk. paper)
    1. Religion—Philosophy. I. Title.
    BL51.J63 2007
    200—dc22

                                                                    2007020036

Printed and bound in the United States of America on acid-free paper that meets the standards of the American National Standard for Permanence of Paper for Printed Library Materials.

Designed and Typeset by Straight Creek Bookmakers.

12 11 10 09 08   1 2 3 4 5

Contents

Part 3: Human Dignity

Preface

Germany is a bi-confessional country. For a long time, its religious landscape was dominated by regional monopolies of either the Catholic or Protestant Church. Both churches regularly organize separate church congresses; the first such congress organized by both churches *together* took place in Berlin in the year 2003. This meeting is rightly considered a historic event in German religious history; more than 100,000 people took part in it. The organizers of this so-called Ecumenical Church Congress invited me to give one of the "main lectures," and they wanted me to deal with an intriguing question. It is this question that inspired the title of the present work: Do we need religion?

The first chapter of the present volume reproduces the text of the "main lecture" I gave on this occasion in Berlin's Deutschlandhalle. This brief text contains almost all the important motifs elaborated on more fully in the book's other chapters. My aim throughout the book is to repudiate all purely functional arguments with respect to faith; to counter such arguments, I point, in direct continuation of my book *The Genesis of Values,* to the importance of experiences of self-transcendence. These experiences cannot, of course, go uninterpreted; moreover, their interpretation does not simply grow out of them. A religious interpretation is in fact even constitutive of some experiences of this kind; I therefore speak of "sacramental" experiences in such cases. Furthermore, religious interpretations do not simply cope with the contingencies of our existence, they change the ways we deal with them. Under conditions of great contingency, the idea of universal human dignity is best able to facilitate the development of shared and binding values.

The task of the next chapter, "Religion in the Age of Contingency," is to cast greater light on the sociological side of this area of problems. The point of departure for my reflections here is the extremely influential diagnosis produced by sociologist of religion Peter Berger, according to whom modern religious and cultural pluralism is loosening individuals' attachment to values and faith and thus contributing to secularization. I counter this diagnosis with historical, sociological, and psycho-philosophical arguments. This leads me to shift the terms of the debate itself—away from a primary focus on the problems of social integration and toward the risks and opportunities of religious pluralism and mounting contingency.

Because the relationship between religious experience and its interpretation demands rather more precise clarification than the opening chapter is able to provide, a study of the problem of the "articulation" of experiences follows. I refer here particularly to the work of the great Franco-Greek philosopher Cornelius Castoriadis (1922–1997). Castoriadis was certainly no philosopher of religion; for him, religion was heteronomy, which he countered with his passionate philosophy of human autonomy. However, building on the work of his philosophical teacher, Maurice Merleau-Ponty, he developed ideas relating to how our experience and its articulation influence and determine one another that are of such profundity that they can yield fruitful results for a theory of religion.

Whereas the three chapters mentioned so far are presented under the rubric of "religious experience," the next five deal with the borderlands between theology and the social sciences. The chapter "Sociology and the Sacred" provides an overview of key texts in the sociology of religion; it was originally written in response to a request by the journal *Merkur*, which, with its amazingly fine ear for the fluctuations of the Zeitgeist, published a special issue, "Inquiring into God—On the Religious Dimension," in 1999. This was partly intended to document the state of the debate in theology and, through my contribution, in the sociology of religion. A sometimes highly critical examination of the English theologian John Milbank follows. In Germany, Milbank is well known only among theologians; in the English-speaking world, meanwhile, his book *Theology and Social Theory*, which first appeared in 1990, has run to many editions and is the subject of heated debates. The next two chapters are dedicated to perhaps the two most important Christian philosophers of our time. The first grapples with the recent work of the Canadian Charles Taylor. Since achieving global fame as a result of his 1989 magnum opus *Sources of the Self,* he has more clearly acknowledged the Catholic motifs in his thought. The second is a portrait of French Protestant philosopher Paul Ricoeur, which I wrote on the occasion of his ninetieth birthday in 2003—once again for *Merkur.* Here, this portrait has been extended to include critical reflection on the relationship between religious experience and its interpretation in Ricoeur's work, particularly with respect to his strong accentuation of the study of the Holy Scriptures for the religious life of individuals and communities. This section of the book concludes with my response to Jürgen Habermas's spectacular acceptance speech as winner of the German book trade's Peace Prize. The focus here is on what the buzzword *post-secular society,* which Habermas has cast into the debate, might actually mean and whether Habermas has really sufficiently and convincingly overhauled his once-radical version of secularization theory.

The third section gathers together texts on the idea of universal human dignity or, to echo the words of the great French sociologist Émile Durkheim, the advancing sacralization of the person under the conditions of modern societies. It begins with an analysis of the work of the Israeli philosopher Avishai Margalit. Here, I explain my doubts about purely "negative" attempts to justify the ideal of human dignity, characteristic of Margalit's work as well as Michael Ignatieff's influential writings on this topic. I also indicate how I myself proceed—by shifting the argument away from purely rational (ultimate) justification toward the blending of such justification with narrative reflection on the genesis of values in general and of the value of human dignity in particular. The brief contribution that follows on the bioethics debate reflects how difficult it is becoming to put the ideal of universal human dignity into practice during a new phase of heightened contingency. The concluding chapter is taken from the Guardini Lectures, which I gave in the spring of 2002 at Humboldt University in Berlin, under the title "The Sacredness of the Person." In this chapter, I grapple with what is surely the most ambitious attempt, made on the threshold of the twentieth century, to investigate the affinity between the structures of modern societies and the belief in human dignity: Émile Durkheim's sociology and his political commentaries. This furnishes me with the opportunity to outline at least some of these affinities between the processes of modernization and the "sacralization" of the person and also to counter an easy optimism based upon it, which appears reckless in light of twentieth-century history. I call into question Durkheim's project, which aims to over-come religious traditions by means of a new "religion de l'humanité." But at the same time, I acknowledge the pressure to reinterpret such religious traditions, including Christianity, that comes from the ad-vancing institutionalization of the value of universal human dignity and that applies to political and moral but also theological issues. Such a reinterpretation goes right to the heart of Christian thought. It is here that more work needs to be done.

This book is a collection of essays; it brings together eleven chap-ters on the topic of religion and commitment to values, which I wrote after completing my book *The Genesis of Values* and while preparing a book on the origins of human rights and the idea of universal human dignity, in other words between 1998 and 2003. All these pieces were written for specific occasions and have been revised only slightly for the present compilation.

The stimulus for publishing these disparate works of mine in coherent form came from Karl Kardinal Lehmann; I am very grateful to him for this and for encouraging me in a number of ways. Of the many Catholic and Protestant interlocutors with whom I discussed these texts in Germany, the United States, and elsewhere, I would like to mention with tremendous gratitude just two whose support and friendship are particularly important to me: Susanna Schmidt, former director of the Catholic Academy in Berlin, and Wolfgang Huber, the Protestant bishop of Berlin and Brandenburg and chairman of the Council of the Protestant Church in Germany. I owe my wife, Heidrun, a debt of gratitude for her great interest, particularly in this aspect of my work, and for her many suggestions on how to improve my arguments. And I am grateful to Christian Scherer for his help in correcting the proofs and preparing the index.

PART 1

Religious Experience

I

Do We Need Religion?

"Embarrassing Incident" is the title of a poem by Bertolt Brecht from the year 1943.[1] Written in his Californian exile, it gives an account of a major celebration among German émigrés on the occasion of the sixty-fifth birthday of Brecht's friend and admired colleague Alfred Döblin, whom he calls in this poem one of his "most revered gods." The birthday celebration took place in a small theater in Santa Monica close to Hollywood, and they had all come: Brecht and his wife, Helene Weigel, Heinrich and Thomas Mann, Lion Feuchtwanger, and Hanns Eisler, who had composed a special piece for this occasion, and the great actors Fritz Kortner, Peter Lorre, and Alexander Granach, all three of whom read from Döblin's books.[2] This tribute to the impoverished and isolated Döblin, who had been a leading novelist and leftist political writer in the Weimar Republic, was going just as well as its organizers had planned. But suddenly the unexpected happened. Döblin began his speech of thanks. He announced that he, the Jewish intellectual, had found his way to the Christian faith and been baptized as a Catholic. Brecht captured this occurrence as follows:

> Then the celebrated god himself stepped onto the platform
>   reserved for artists
> And declared in a loud voice
> Right in front of my sweat-drenched friends and students
> That he had just been afflicted with an illumination and now
> Had become religious and with unseemly haste

> He provocatively clapped a moth-eaten cleric's bonnet
>   on his head
> Fell lewdly to his knees and shamelessly
> Struck up a saucy hymn, thus offending
> The irreligious sentiments of his listeners, some of them
> Mere youths.
> For the last three days
> I haven't dared show my face
> Among my friends and students
> I'm so
> Embarrassed.

This episode provides us with an initial answer to the question I am posing today. Religiosity—in one possible translation of Brecht's response—is a sign of weakness. Human beings are in need of religion only when they are too weak to live without it. Although the tone of the poem is more or less malicious, Brecht was certainly capable of treating his friend with greater empathy. In his journals,[3] he articulates "the sympathetic horror felt when a fellow prisoner succumbs to torture and talks," and he adduces the many terrible blows of fate that had brought matters to such a pass and that must be considered extenuating circumstances: the loss of two sons, lack of success, illness, and problems in his marriage. For Brecht, all this explains Döblin's conversion as a breakdown, but the basic idea clearly remains the same: To be religious means to be weak, and one should not yield to such weakness, at least not publicly. One's friends are embarrassed if one shows one's weakness in broad daylight.

Döblin is unlikely ever to have seen Brecht's poem, but the embarrassment and outrage felt by his friends, some of whom caused a stir by leaving the celebration early, and the cooling of his friendship with Brecht can surely not have escaped him. The views of Döblin's leftist kindred spirits were quite out of sync with his own self-esteem. In literary terms, Döblin was as prolific as ever; the power of his language and even the brash Berlin tone, which continued to feature in many of his commentaries, do not suggest a broken man. In a similar set of circumstances, he ironically fends off the insinuation that he became a believer because of illness, stating: "I am not sick, I was not sick, and I will never be sick."[4] And he wrote a powerful dialogue on religion because he wanted to translate Christianity "into his own language." Here, he distinguished between two types of weakness, as if to counter the interpretations of his friends: The first entails "declining strength," the second "waning resistance."[5] Thus for him, it was the other way around: Those who flee from their relationship with God and indulge in false certainties are the weak ones.

What do we feel when we look back on this "embarrassing incident" today, more than sixty years later? Is it not Brecht's response itself that we find embarrassing, because it reveals the embarrassing certainty of Brecht's own beliefs? His faith was not, of course, a faith in God, but there is no doubt that Brecht felt he knew the answer to questions about the meaning of life, and this answer was political. He assumed that the laws of history had been discovered by the science of Marxism and that human history would progress until communism itself had been achieved. But does this "faith in history" not seem very aged today? Was not the term *scientific communism,* used in communist countries to refer to an academic discipline and academic posts at universities and colleges, the butt of jokes long before the collapse of the regimes in Eastern Europe? One could not go on forever blaming the failure to realize utopian dreams on unfavorable conditions. When the colossus that was the Soviet Union collapsed, it had definitely become impossible to deny that the focus of contemporary problems had shifted. Few, however, grasped just how profound these historical upheavals were.

Not only Marxists but almost all influential social scientists and historical thinkers had for long assumed that secularization, in the sense of the decline of religion, is a necessary corollary of modernization. We need only glance at the world around us to find this assumption seemingly confirmed at every turn. There have always been exceptions, such as Poland and Ireland, but these were quickly explained away with handy theories. The most difficult case has always been the United States. Nobody could deny that it is a modern society, yet religion has remained a vigorous force, not only in the shape of Protestant fundamentalism but in a rich plurality of forms.[6] This is why the United States has been treated as a very special case, as a modern society in a religious third world, as some commentators have put it. But the perspective of sociologists of religion has changed dramatically even in this respect. As large parts of the world outside of those areas molded by Christianity modernize rapidly, a huge experiment is taking place before our eyes. This allows us to investigate empirically the relationship between secularization and modernization. The provisional findings make it more plausible to classify Europe—rather than the United States—as the exceptional case. Secularization as Europe has experienced it is not simply being repeated today on a global scale. Some authors therefore even speak of desecularization. Whatever the precise outcome of this research, there are good reasons to question the assumption that religion in all its diversity is set to disappear—without, however, simply presenting this as evidence that religion is a universal, an anthropological given that can only be suppressed by force.

I think this is a fair characterization of the present historical period, in which we ask: Do we need religion? If those who see religion as superfluous and dangerous, as well as believers who assume that without faith there is only decline and decadence, have both lost their certainty, this could be a favorable moment for a new way of thinking.

I certainly do not believe we can answer our question by pointing to advantages of one kind or another that an individual, society, or mankind might glean from religion. Some claim that only believers can be truly happy or consistently moral or psychologically healthy; only if people believe can societies be peacefully integrated and considerate toward minority groups. All this may be true; I personally tend to assume that some of these claims are plausible. But in every individual case, our reason compels us to investigate the alleged causal connections in an objective manner. We must never simply take a causal connection for granted because it chimes with the enthusiastic certainties of belief. Reflecting on the functional advantages and beneficial effects of religion in this way can lead to interesting research. Yet it brings us no closer to the point that those who ask "Do we need religion?" want to reach. For one thing seems to me indubitable. Whatever the results of such research, even the most perfect proof of the utility of religious belief cannot cause anybody to hold such a belief. Nobody can believe because he has been convinced by rational means that believing is useful, that it serves a purpose. If we apply notions of religious utility to ourselves, we end up with Pascal's famous wager. But we all know that the result of such cold, rational calculation would inspire little emotional intensity. What is more, as William James once wrote, God would not be taken in by such rational calculations. "And if we were ourselves in the place of the Deity, we should probably take particular pleasure in cutting off believers of this pattern from this infinite reward."[7] If notions of utility with regard to religion are applied to societies as a whole, this inevitably gives rise to a division between an elite that knows better and the masses who supposedly need belief to pacify them. The famous quip "I am an atheist, but Catholic of course" comes from the radical Right in France about a century ago (Maurice Barrès) and articulates this thinking in a particularly cynical way.

This means that we have to conceive of the "need" in our question in a different way. "Need" relates not to the external purpose of a belief, its usefulness. It must refer to something inherent in belief. It must be bound up with the experience we call belief. The question is not "Is religion useful?" but "Can we live without the experience articulated in faith, in religion?" If this is the right question, then we have to look more closely at what kind of experience this is and in which forms we might encounter it.

I therefore propose that we reflect on those kinds of experience that are not yet experiences of the divine, but without which we cannot understand what faith, what religion, is. I call them experiences of self-transcendence. This means experiences in which a person transcends herself, but not, at least not immediately, in the sense of moral achievements but rather of being pulled beyond the boundaries of one's self, being captivated by something outside of myself, a relaxation of or liberation from one's fixation on oneself. We thus initially define this self-transcendence only as a movement away from oneself, as the somewhat antiquated German word *Ergriffensein* expresses quite beautifully.

There is no doubt that we do have such experiences. My book *The Genesis of Values*[8] was an attempt to offer, together with philosophical and social psychological reflections on the precise character of this self-transcendence, a rich phenomenology of such experiences. You will be familiar with all of them. I invite you to read one description without succumbing to the suspicion that I am merely identifying religious faith with such experiences. Yet we can assuredly *approach* belief through such experiences.

In Knut Hamsun's novel *Mysteries,* a man named Nagel walks into a forest. Here is what he experiences:

> A tremor of ecstasy ran through him. He felt himself carried away and engulfed by the magic rays of the sun. The stillness filled him with an intoxicating sense of well-being; he was free from worry; the only sound was a soft murmur from above, the hum of the universal machinery—God turning his treadmill.

> Not a leaf stirred in the trees—not a pine needle dropped. Nagel hugged his knees in sheer delight; he felt exhilarated because life was good. It beckoned to him and he responded. He raised himself on his elbow and looked around him. There wasn't a soul in sight. He said yes to life once more and listened, but no one came. Again he said yes, but there was no answer.
>
> Strange; he had distinctly heard someone calling him. But he dismissed the thought; perhaps he had imagined the whole thing. But nothing was going to shatter his joyful mood. He was in a strange, euphoric state of mind; his every nerve vibrated; music surged through his blood; he was part of nature, of the sun, the mountains; he was omniscient; the trees, the earth, the moss, spoke to him alone. His soul went into a crescendo, like an organ with all the stops pulled out. Never would he forget how this heavenly music would pulsate through his blood.[9]

Here we have all the attributes of an experience of self-transcendence in an experience of ecstatic fusion with nature. Our interaction with other human beings might involve similar experiences. Think of a conversation that goes beyond the exchange of trivialities, information, or argument, during which you suddenly have the feeling that your interlocutor has intuitively understood deep layers of your personality, giving you the courage to talk about the formative events in your life and, perhaps, about stirrings you yourself have as yet scarcely acknowledged. Such a conversation also represents the experience of transcending the boundaries of one's self, an experience you will remember and that leaves behind some affective attachment to one's interlocutor, making it easier to interact next time around. We have the same experience, felt with far greater intensity, when we fall in love or are in love with another person. This strong feeling of closeness has for long and in many cultures been interpreted as a *renewal* of a relationship, as if one had known the other before, or forever, or as if one's ancestors or God had meant it to be thus. This expresses the force—for which no other explanation seems to be available—with which two human beings, often after just a few moments, are drawn to each other, recognize themselves in the other, and find themselves accepted by the other. We experience third parties' enquiries as to what we find so attractive about the loved partner as inappropriate, because we are not falling in love with specific properties or attributes but with a whole person for whom there is no rational denominator. Sexual experiences, one might say, combine the experience of fusion with another person with fusion with nature: We can experience mutual understanding but also the enjoyment of the beauty of another's body, the joy of knowing that one's own body is experienced as beautiful and loved, and a sensual pleasure that goes beyond the quotidian and is one of the strongest foundations of deeply felt human relationships.

No impenetrable wall separates experiences of selflessness and overcoming of the self, in the context of love for one's fellows and charity, from eros. Here, too, a phenomenology can begin with rather trivial experiences, such as the pleasure of giving and the fact that there is probably nobody who always thinks only of himself and his own advantage, although self-love is frequently extended only to a narrow circle, such as one's family, and the fixation on one's self remains intact. But the experiences of helping and receiving help can be experiences of self-transcendence. This is true of the experience of being shocked by others' neediness, be they our loved ones or even anonymous others. The beggar we ignore on ninety-nine out of a hundred days or to whom we make a small donation to quiet our vaguely bad conscience might suddenly be experienced as our *brother*—although this term is too well-worn to really get across the shattering character of an experience that brings home to you the fact that the other truly is an ego like you and that you could be in his shoes, leading his life in his body.

Here, we encounter the voice of morality in the experience of being deeply moved, although erotic love, which demands a certain permanence, also produces obligations, and even the intense experience of nature has repercussions for how we deal with nature and for our moral conceptions of what constitutes an appropriate relationship with nature. In the shattering of one's self by the other, some thinkers have seen the root of all morality, and there is no doubt that many moral emotions like shame and outrage feature an intense experience of self-transcendence. Finally, we must turn our attention to the experiences of collective ecstasy that arise when groups of people begin to feel fired up, as we say metaphorically; when the individual's self-control diminishes to such an extent that she becomes overconfident and engages in activities she would otherwise consider beyond her capabilities. Speakers become funnier when they sense that their words are being well received, or grandiloquent when they sense agreement and support. We feel stronger, smarter, or more beautiful, or perhaps, when masked or dressed up, like completely different beings, just as others seem transformed by a mysterious, anonymous force. This transformation might make us generous. We might give away our money, as many did spontaneously in Berlin in November 1989. Or it might make us aggressive and violent, prone to pogroms and massacres, united against those we experience as a threat to our ecstatic union. Clearly, not all experiences of self-transcendence are morally good. But we have to be willing, at least initially, to look in a "value-free" way at all experiences that tie human beings to values, whatever these values are, even if we despise them or find them worthless, dangerous, or evil.

However, it is not only disturbing social phenomena of this kind, in which the experience of self-transcendence might occur or to which it might lead, which make problematic what might have seemed for a moment a kitsch and overly harmonious panegyric on the miracles of nature, eros, and charity. Not all experiences of self-transcendence are rousing. We can also be shaken by suffering, including our own suffering. For rousing experiences of every type, there exists a "terrible equivalent": We might experience not only enthusiasm about nature but also horror at nature, *Naturgrauen* (Arthur Schnitzler), not only the building of trust and commitment but also the loss of trust and betrayal, not only falling in love but the loss of a loved one through separation or death, not only ecstatic sexual union but also rape. Just as we can feel pulled beyond ourselves into unprecedented joy, we can also be shocked to discover how vulnerable we always are, how finite everything to which we are attached in fact is, and how incurably precarious our existence is. Asking whether we need such experiences is as pointless as it is in the case of rousing experiences. We simply have them. Life without them is unimaginable, even were we to rid ourselves of all the havoc wrought by human beings.

Paul Tillich wrote in a particularly sensitive manner of the experience of anxiety as an experience of self-transcendence. Anxiety, says Tillich, is "finitude, experienced as one's own finitude."[10] Note the word *experienced* here. Tillich is explicitly not referring to an abstract knowledge that we have always possessed. What he means here "is not the realization of universal transitoriness, not even the experience of the death of others, but the impression of these events on the always latent awareness of our own having to die . . . " This produces anxiety, naked anxiety, which we can only bear for short moments; rational discourse can gain as little purchase on this as it can on the experience of love. A phenomenology of anxiety is thus a necessary component of any phenomenology of self-transcendence. Following Tillich, we would distinguish between three types of anxiety that haunt us as relative or absolute threats to our feeling of existence. We can be relatively threatened by the blows of fate and absolutely threatened in the face of death. We can experience a relative emptiness intellectually and spiritually, and we can also experience the world as completely meaningless: Every aspect of the world that might appeal to us and motivate us to act is lost to us in our depressive state. We might feel relatively threatened in terms of our self-understanding as moral beings because of a feeling of guilt caused by our actions or failure to act. But we can also fall apart entirely because of our tremendous guilt, for which we can never make amends, and because of the prospect of eternal condemnation.

Tillich didn't doubt that these experiences of anxiety can lead to faith. "Only those who have experienced the shock of transitoriness, the anxiety in which they are aware of their finitude, the threat of nonbeing, can understand what the notion of God means. Only those who have experienced the tragic ambiguities of our historical existence and have totally questioned the meaning of existence can understand what the symbol of the Kingdom of God means."[11]

Those for whom faith is the result of weakness—like Döblin's alienated political friends mentioned at the beginning of this chapter—might see this as confirming their view. But things are not so simple: Apart from anything else, we must bear in mind the rousing experiences that inspire adherence to certain values. These are as capable of forming a bridge to faith as are experiences of anxiety. What these experiences have in common is self-transcendence. We encounter in them a power that wrenches us beyond ourselves, even if this means, as in the case of anxiety, that we become aware of our limits. But this awareness of limits entails the feeling of "absolute dependence" (Schleiermacher's *schlechthinnige Abhängigkeit*): As we undergo rousing experiences, we become the grateful recipients of undeserved gifts.

The matter at hand is less simple than it might seem for another particularly important reason. Faith does not simply *emanate* from either rousing or anxious experiences. Religion articulates such experiences of self-transcendence, but it does so in a specific manner. For the believer, the experience of being deeply moved is the experience of an unconditional and unavailable other. But this does not apply to the nonbeliever. Neither does it apply to all believers in the same way. Therefore, having talked so much about experience, we must now turn to its interpretation. If there is no question that we undergo such experiences, what of their interpretation? Do we need to interpret them religiously?

Nonreligious people will tend to consider all the experiences I have mentioned to be purely psychological phenomena. Whereas the believer will feel grateful for creation as he experiences nature and will see love among humans as reflecting the splendor of divine love and the blows of fate perhaps as punishment or at least God's unfathomable providence, the nonbeliever will classify such experiences as the psychological processing of mere accidents, whether happy or unhappy, or of the inevitable fate of all living beings. There is, at first sight, not much to criticize here because these phenomena certainly are psychological in nature. But the question is whether we are justified in stating that they are *nothing but* psychological phenomena, as if classifying these experiences resolves the question of their origin. But just as the believer cannot compel the nonbeliever to accept his religious interpretation on the basis of logic, the nonbeliever cannot advocate his nonreligious interpretation as the only rationally defensible one. Here, a gap opens up between experience and interpretation, which we must look at more closely.

Three observations might be helpful. First, subjectively, specific interpretations of our experience frequently appear to be the only possible or plausible ones. Although the observer might perceive a difference between experience and interpretation, this is not always so for the experiencing subject herself. We might have the experience of a (subjective) "revelation" when, for example, we suddenly find the right word that turns the sense of a gap in what had been said before into a specific experience. With regard to all the other interpretations of our experience, even our own descriptions, we might have had a nagging sense of inadequacy. But now, suddenly, everything has become clear to us; experience is completely transformed into expression. When we have this experience, interpretation and experience are indissolubly fused for us. We are then very hesitant even to discuss our interpretations.

Second, the process of articulating experiences can start at both ends. Sometimes we encounter the right word that allows us to admit for the first time that this is the experience we once had. In this sense, languages, cultures, and religions are rich repertoires for the articulation of experiences. The existing interpretive models are permeated with experience, just as our experiences are dependent on interpretations and expectations.[12]

Third, and most important, specific interpretations might be the precondition for certain experiences. In the realm of religious experience, this is absolutely crucial. We might cut ourselves off from certain experiences if we give precedence to skepticism. The classical elaboration of this notion is found in William James's essay "The Will to Believe." Here, too, we should think first of all of such things as falling in love and mutual confidence-building. He who waits, cold and aloof, to obtain from the other a sure sign of love usually waits in vain. I have to meet the other halfway and be willing to trust her and at the same time be convinced that I am, in principle, worthy of the other's love. For love to arise, I must consider myself worthy of love and the other capable of love. Love demands a leap in the dark. The same goes for religious faith. The injunction to believe only what we encounter in ordinary experience would cut us off from extraordinary experiences—but why should we cut ourselves off in this way, giving precedence to fear over hope? If our attitude to the world alters how the world is expressed, there is no compelling reason to confront the world without faith. To have certain experiences we must be willing to believe.

This is immediately evident in the case of prayer. Prayers turn the opening-up of oneself toward something higher—the experience of self-transcendence—into an activity. Although we must be able to listen if we want to pray, we are also allowed to speak and to turn toward an Other that transcends every concretely human other. William James thought that nobody abstains entirely from praying, that every human being prays whether or not he admits this in terms of his particular worldview. He came to this conclusion because he thought that every self demands an ideal Other that cannot be found among human beings. I do not know whether this is true. I am not even sure how we would investigate it. But James's statement is certainly true if it means that prayer is that type of religious activity that requires almost no theological foundation. Praying, at least in its elementary forms, is a continuation of an activity of which all human beings are capable.

This does not apply to another type of experience, which I would like to call "sacramental." The Eucharist, or the Lord's Supper, is for many Christian believers a very intense religious experience, but self-evidently the consumption of bread and wine becomes an extraordinary experience only if the participant has a basic knowledge

of the faith and the meaning of this ritual. This ritual clearly picks up
on elements of everyday life that point somewhat beyond the ordinary,
such as a shared meal and a celebration. But it goes radically beyond
the ordinary if we grasp its religious meaning. It would be misleading
to treat sacramental experiences as if they were nothing but religious
interpretations of universally accessible experiences. Here, interpretations are the preconditions for the experience. If we try to convey
these experiences to nonbelievers, we will, of course, compare them
with experiences accessible to them; some have, for example, boldly
attempted to relate the experience of the Eucharist to ecstatic sexual
experiences (André Dubus).[13] Some might view this as scandalous,
whereas others will see here the mutual reflection of different kinds of
love. But everyone is aware that such attempts at description are never
more than approximations of the qualities experienced, and that the
experience itself depends on having been trained to have it.

If this is so, religious traditions and institutions are not only
rich repertoires of interpretations vis-à-vis our experiences of self-
transcendence, but they enable us to have such experiences in the
first place. They contain knowledge of a physical character relating
to how we can prepare ourselves for such experiences—through as-
cetic practices, through certain bodily postures, such as kneeling, by
singing and making music together. More importantly, knowledge of
faith can in fact help us overcome the centering of our experience on
ourselves. Experiences of self-transcendence really have to be experiences of decentering rather than attempts made by a self that fully
intends to remain itself but would also like to enjoy the titillation of
extraordinary experiences.

Some will harbor this suspicion anyway if, as is the case here, we
place so much emphasis on religious experience. They might think
that faith loses its seriousness, as well as its beauty, when interpreted
through the subjective experiences of the believers. This danger
of tailoring faith to the logic of an "experiential society" (Gerhard
Schulze) certainly exists. The sociology of religion features discussions
of increasing religious "bricolage" and "patchwork identities," that is,
highly subjective combinations of elements from different religious
traditions: a little bit of Christianity, for example, with a pinch of Bud-
dhism and a dash of esotericism. Everybody then has his own belief,
all binding force is gone, even as regards the individual, belief and
belonging are decoupled, and there are as many religious persuasions
as there are individuals. All the theological objections raised against

this complete subjectivism are justified. Faith of this kind fails to cast off the shackles of narcissist self-centeredness and is deployed only in specific situations, like a hobby for which there is never enough time, owing to the constraints of everyday life. A private language[14] merely allows dialogue with oneself; intensification of belief is a more earnest undertaking than its extensification. But we should not overdo this criticism. Such combining can entail creative and productive potential. We should bear in mind that the history of Christianity is far from a linear and homogeneous tradition. Religious virtuosi have always enriched the spiritual heritage of Christianity. Meister Eckhart was inspired by elements of Judaism; Saint Francis probably drew on elements of Islam. Both integrated these into Christianity. Neither should we forget that religious patchworks are not as new in religious history as they might seem. Denominational boundaries have frequently been rather blurred in the minds of believers, and one can often identify the traces of pre-Christian and non-Christian religiosity in the regional variants of this faith. We should therefore exercise caution before rushing to condemn, remaining open to the potential of individualism to help vitalize religious life.

How do these reflections on the relationship between interpretation and experience in the sphere of religion help us answer our original question? We have discovered that all human beings are in principle capable of having experiences of self-transcendence. Believers interpret these experiences in light of their beliefs. For them, this must mean that God can be experienced even by those who do not attribute their experiences to God—those who hear something different from believers when they hear the word *God*. Moreover, we have seen that faith makes certain experiences possible, experiences from which the nonbeliever cuts herself off. But all of us have to cut ourselves off from some interpretations and experiences; criticism is a part of interpretation, not external to it. It therefore behooves us to be modest in our relationship to other religions. At least to some extent, we have to consider them attempts, often very impressive ones, to interpret human experiences of the divine. The belief in Jesus Christ is thus grounded in a relationship to God accessible to all men. "If we were Atheists without Jesus, Jesus himself could not liberate us from our atheism, because we would not have an organ to receive him" (Paul Tillich).[15] But this modesty must also extend to those who are not followers of another religious belief but who profess no faith at all. There certainly exists a profound kind of atheism, an attitude of unbelief that develops into a fervor for the love of others and the world as a whole. Our reflections lead us to conclude merely that those ways of thinking are harmful that allow no interpretation of experiences of self-transcendence, forcing us to remain silent about them and preventing us from entering into communication with the divine. These are harmful because they hinder human profundity and keep us fixated on ourselves. Religious faith thus increases the probability that an individual will have experiences of the kind here described, and, if she has them, does not repress them. It increases the probability that one will grow beyond a mere morality of prudence, respect that which is unavailable, and find the strength and stamina to change the world. But this is a falsifiable empirical statement, not triumphalist self-adulation. Religion in general and the Christian faith in particular cannot be made logically compelling. Christians can only offer their faith and invite others to follow Christ. We are more likely to succeed in converting others if we convert ourselves, if we live the faith that we are proclaiming, and that we need—rather than explaining to others why they *ought* to need it.

Thus, although there is such a thing as profound atheism, there is also superficial faith or, worse, faith as a false comfort. Some people have difficulties with faith, because they assume that being a believer obliges them to see a beneficial act in every blow of fate. They protest against pseudo-rational consolation precisely because they wish to protect the authenticity of their feelings. Even some believers praise their faith and our dependence on religion by arguing that this is the only way to resolve questions for which science and philosophy have no answers. Even great thinkers like Max Weber thought that religions must be understood mainly as attempts to solve the problem of theodicy, that is, the question of why God allows evil and suffering.

But is such an understanding of religion appropriate, particularly with regard to Christianity? Everyone in Germany knows Paul Gerhardt's wonderful hymn "O Sacred Head Sore Wounded." Listen to the following verse:

> My Savior, be Thou near me when death is at my door;
> Then let Thy presence cheer me, forsake me nevermore!
> When soul and body languish, oh, leave me not alone,
> But take away mine anguish by virtue of Thine own!

The sensational thing about this, if you will allow me this colloquialism, is the last line. When push comes to shove, the Christian believer does not expect consolation and help from a great hero who was himself persecuted, but who easily triumphed over his enemies by dint of his superior powers. Rather, the Christian turns to one who has been through the whole ordeal himself and finds consolation in this very fact. Why though, fearing death, should we find consolation in remembering another's fear of death? Why does this lessen our own fear? It does not simply disappear and make way for a feeling of foolhardy invincibility. Yet my belief that God Himself suffered my fear when he took human form enables me to integrate my fear or anxiety into my courage to live. Faith enables me to articulate my experiences of fear and anxiety and to experience afresh salvation through divine love again and again. The emphasis in this sentence is on this "freshness." If we see faith as a fixed source of rational consolation, as the definitive answer to our questions, we deprive it of the dynamism bound up with this freshness.

What has been said here with regard to the experience of fear and anxiety and all experiences of self-transcendence is also true of morality and history. Moral dilemmas do not disappear by virtue of faith, as if God had decided that there can be no conflicts between values or between moral obligations among believers. Neither do the tragic aspects of history vanish, as if there were only one grandiose history of salvation in which all the horrors and failures make perfect sense.

Biblically, this is expressed in the Psalms, among other things. Jesus's cry, "My God, my God, why have you forsaken me?" clearly underlies Paul Gerhardt's hymn. But this cry itself refers back to Psalm 22, which begins with these words. This lamentation of godforsakenness is directed at God, a God, in fact, addressed as "my God" through a specifically personal grammatical form. Is it a contradiction in itself to lament through prayer that one has been forsaken by God? Can such lamentation take the form of prayer in the first place?

At the present time, when people tend to doubt that God exists rather than questioning His love and affection for us, lamentation as prayer might seem paradoxical. But for the believer, the psalm offers the opportunity to communicate with God about one's very doubts and to implore Him to help us reconstruct our shattered confidence in Him. For the believer, this means that God does not expect blind obedience from us and constant tacit consent. In fact, the tone of Psalm 22 changes dramatically after the lengthy verses of lamentation:

But be not thou far from me, O Lord;
O my strength, haste thee to help me,
Deliver my soul from the sword,
My darling from the power of the dog.
Save me from the lion's mouth;
For thou hast heard me from the horns of the unicorns.
I will declare thy name unto my brethren;
In the midst of the congregation will I praise thee.

After this change of tone, the psalm goes on to praise God and features a declaration of intent to make sacrifices and to tell everyone about God.

Paul Ricoeur, the great French Christian philosopher, interprets this passage[16]—in the book *Penser la bible*—as a means of balancing things out subsequent to the narrative of salvation and the prophets' moralization of our actions. This idea seems to me an exact parallel to my own thesis that morality and history look different if we eschew thinking about them holistically and make room for value pluralism and historical tragedy. We will certainly always have to work to achieve moral consistency and to narrate a comprehensive story. But the vantage point from which we do so will always be a new and unique situation of action and suffering. To deal with this situation, without false certainties, believers trust in God. They cannot live without the experience of being able to offer to God all their rejoicing, all sorrows, and even all their doubts, receiving help that might not always come in the form they originally expected. In this sense, believers need their belief. And they offer nonbelievers the opportunity to discover the same thing for themselves.

NOTES

1. Bertolt Brecht, "Peinlicher Vorfall," in *Gesammelte Werke,* vol. 10 (Frankfurt am Main: Suhrkamp, 1967), 861f. Thanks to David Dollenmayer (Worcester Polytechnic Institute) for his help in translating this poem.

2. See Werner Mittenzwei, *Das Leben des Bertolt Brecht,* vol. 2 (Berlin [GDR]: Aufbau, 1986), 106ff.

3. Bertolt Brecht, *Arbeitsjournal,* entry of August 14, 1943 (Frankfurt am Main: Suhrkamp, 1973).

4. Alfred Döblin, letter to Wilhelm Hausenstein of January 31, 1947, in *Briefe* (Olten: Walter, 1970), 364.

5. Alfred Döblin, *Der unsterbliche Mensch. Ein Religionsgespräch* (Munich: Deutscher Taschenbuch Verlag, 1992; originally published in 1946), 161.

6. See the chapter "Religion in the Age of Contingency" in this volume.

7. William James, *The Will to Believe and Other Essays in Popular Philosophy* (New York: Longmans, Green & Co., 1897), 1–31, esp. 6.

8. Hans Joas, *The Genesis of Values* (Chicago: University of Chicago Press, 2003), 41.

9. Knut Hamsun, *Mysteries,* trans. Gerry Bothmer (New York: Farrar, Strauss and Giroux, 1971), 64f.

10. Paul Tillich, *The Courage to Be* (New Haven, CT: Yale University Press, 1952), 35.

11. Paul Tillich, *Systematic Theology,* 4th ed., vol. 1 (Chicago: University of Chicago Press, 1955), 61f.

12. On these points, see the chapter "On the Articulation of Experience" in this volume.

13. See André Dubus, *Adultery and Other Choices* (Boston: David R. Godine, 1977), 168ff.

14. Richard Schröder, "Wie beim Handy, so beim Glauben: 'Wechseln Sie einfach den Anbieter!' Funktioniert das?" *Chrismon* 5 (2003): 46.

15. Paul Tillich, *Gesammelte Werke,* vol. 8 (Stuttgart: Evangelisches Verlagswerk, 1970), 93.

16. Paul Ricoeur and André LaCocque, *Penser la bible* (Paris: Seuil, 1998), 279ff.

2

Religion in the Age of Contingency

In his book *A Far Glory: The Quest for Faith in an Age of Credulity,*[1] the well-known sociologist of religion and Protestant thinker Peter Berger tells an old American joke:

> Two friends meet on the street in southern California. One looks very unhappy, and the other asks him why. "I now have a job. A terrible job." "What's so terrible about it?" "Well, let me tell you what I have to do. I work in an orange grove. All day long I sit in the shade, under a tree, and these other guys bring me oranges. I put the big ones in one basket, the little ones in a second basket, and the in-between ones in a third basket. And that's what I do all day long." His friend says, "I don't understand. This seems to me like a very pleasant job. What bothers you about it?" To which the first replies, *"All those decisions!"* (175f.)

This joke leads us directly to the topic of religion, contingency, and pluralism. Nobody would deny that the increasing number of options for action open to individuals as a result of modernization increases the number of decisions that have to be made, and that many people experience this not as an expression of their freedom but as a freedom forced on them. The term *contingency* has taken hold to express such paradoxical connections between individual freedom and a sense

21

of coercion. Likewise, nobody would deny that the opportunity to decide, that is, the existence of a certain space of self-determination, leads to a *pluralism* of cultures, subcultures, and individuals or reinforces a preexisting pluralism. But views on how contingency and pluralism relate to one another differ widely, particularly in the sphere of religion. What are the consequences of contingency and pluralism for our commitment to certain values, and for faith, its vitality and transmission?

The interpretations produced by Peter Berger, to whom I owe the joke with which we opened, are particularly influential in both academic and religious circles, although empirical research often fails to confirm them, and the philosophical assumptions on which they are based are deeply problematical. In what follows I use them as a foil to clarify my own interpretations.

Berger's emphasis is not so much on contingency as pluralism. This he defines, in a close approximation of everyday usage, as "the co-existence with a measure of civic peace of different groups in one society" (37). Religious pluralism, then, is "just one of several varieties of the phenomenon"; because the definition of the term *coexistence* requires clarification, he states that "in the present context it implies more than abstaining from mutual slaughter; rather, it denotes a certain degree of social interaction." Berger puts special emphasis on this, because coexistence without interaction, social life featuring insurmountable barriers between groups, could not really, according to Berger, be called pluralism.

Berger is fully aware that modern pluralism is not a historical novelty, although he tends to consider it the exception rather than the rule. He considers our modern pluralism as "uncannily similar" to that of antiquity, particularly the living conditions in the large city-states of "late Hellenistic and Roman times." The only feature truly specific to *modern* pluralism is its extent, as evident in the ever larger and more heterogeneous urban areas of the present era, in which human beings from a vast number of cultures often live at close quarters and encounter one another frequently. The culture of these urban areas, and therefore of pluralism, is increasingly pervading rural areas, if these themselves have not already been almost completely urbanized.

One could start analyzing in precise quantitative terms whether this assumption truly characterizes all cities or regions today. But for Berger, and also for my own project, the sociopsychological dynamics of this pluralism are of far greater import. Berger's work features a number of core assumptions of profound significance in this regard. For him, the peaceful coexistence of cultures and religions, in the absence of major barriers to contact between them, necessarily leads to what he calls "cognitive contamination," a mixture of diverse lifestyles, values, and beliefs. His underlying psychological assumption is that when people encounter other values and worldviews, they inevitably conclude that they can no longer take things for granted as they had done before, and that others might also have a good idea or two. The crack in one's worldview might be tiny in the beginning, but it has a tendency to grow into a chasm. According to Berger, this ultimately leads to pure relativism, which holds that all convictions and values are of equal worth or at least equally unfounded. Application of the economic concept of "preference" to religion, as common among some contemporary sociologists of religion but also in the everyday lives of many Americans, is for Berger a symptom of such creeping relativism. Berger is certainly right in stating that the phrase "religious preference" "belongs to the language of consumer behavior, not to the language of martyrdom" (34). On this view, religious faith as such and each particular faith is treated as a mere option, as purely subjective and transitory. But Berger refrains from rejecting this language; for him, it perfectly captures the facts: "The individual's religion [within the context of modernity] is not something irrevocably given, a *datum* that he can change no more than he can change his genetic inheritance; rather, religion becomes choice, a product of the individual's ongoing project of world- and self-construction" (67). Via these psychological mechanisms, pluralism thus leads to secularization. For Berger, pluralism is not the only factor leading to secularization, but it is certainly an important one. This factor reinforces other factors (such as technological and scientific progress, which for Berger also have secularizing consequences). A spiral is triggered: "Modernity can then be said to bring about an ongoing cross-fertilization of pluralism and secularity" (40).

One key element is missing from my reconstruction of Berger's diagnosis. Subjectivist relativism is for him only one possible result of the "cognitive contamination" mentioned previously. At least with regard to Christian communities, he distinguishes four different types of reaction: The first is a strategy of negotiation, as typical of liberal theology, which makes many cognitive compromises with modernity in order to save the core of the faith; the second, total capitulation, with a complete loss even of that core; the third, withdrawal into the ghetto of believers; and the fourth, a religious crusade to reconquer society in the name of religious tradition. The third and the fourth approaches are important for Berger, because he thinks that relativism is ultimately untenable psychologically: It might at any moment be transformed utterly into fundamentalism, among both individuals and religious communities. I know that many find this assumption highly plausible. However politically conservative he may be, his own stance is in fact liberal from a theological point of view. He often refers to feeling most at home with a middle way between the extremes.

I have not gone into other elements of Berger's sociology of religion, his thesis of the ongoing privatization of religion being the most important. The reason for this is simple. This thesis has been rejected almost completely in recent years, primarily because of the research carried out by José Casanova,[2] and Berger has almost retracted it, at least insofar as privatization is identified with the decline of religion. On February 25, 1968, in the *New York Times,* Berger predicted that there would be no churches or religious communities left by the year 2000, merely small sects in which believers would huddle together to resist a worldwide secular culture. Today, Berger calls this prediction the "big mistake" of his career.[3] But he believes that he has made up for this by coming up with his crucial insight into the causal relationship between pluralism and secularization, as I have sketched it here.

Unfortunately, this has to be seen as another "big mistake." Berger has failed to recognize the internal connection between the thesis he has abandoned and the thesis he still defends, and for which he makes even stronger claims today. Although he has switched from championing radical predictions of secularization to advocating what he now calls "desecularization" theory,[4] he fails to grasp the deeply problematic nature of his theory of the dynamics of pluralism.

I now explain the reasons for this harsh judgment. I see historical, sociological, and philosophical objections to Berger's theoretical construction.

Let us begin with the historical objections. Contrary to Berger, I believe that pluralism has always been an inherent feature of European religious history. Europe was never completely Christian; Judaism and Islam also form part of Europe's heritage. The pre-monotheistic religions never completely disappeared but permeated the later forms of religion. And even the religions of antiquity have exercised a constant subterranean influence on European cultural history. "The existence of a plurality of religious communities at the same time and in the same area has been the rule in European history."[5] Berger's picture of modern pluralism is characterized by an exaggerated historical contrast, which implies that until recently it was common to be surrounded exclusively by coreligionists and to remain unaffected by religious doubts. But this is a complete distortion of European history, similar to the dichotomous contrast in Arnold Gehlen's book *Primitive Man and Late Culture,*[6] which, indeed, greatly influenced Berger's thinking. This theory is based on the idea that the less room for reflection institutions allow, the stronger they are. On this view, if institutions enable people to question them, they become weaker. The internalization of norms and values in such institutions is allegedly superficial and unstable.

But these are the old assumptions of an ultraconservative theory of institutions advocated by practically no one over the last few decades. Even Helmut Schelsky, Gehlen's intellectual alter ego, admitted that a certain freedom to reflect might stabilize institutions.[7] Berger remains skeptical in this regard and fails to recognize how enormously stabilizing it can be to open up institutions to discussion, how the periodic shift between institutional ultra-stability and collapse can be avoided through learning and controlled change. In much the same way, he fails to recognize that the flexible internalization of norms and values is not necessarily superficial. On a personal level, it can facilitate heightened sensitivity toward others and toward the "Other" within me, overcome compulsiveness, and thus engender dynamic (rather than static) stability—just as discourses can on the institutional level.

Berger's views on the destructive consequences of pluralism are influenced by this ultraconservative concept of the institution. The other major weakness in Berger's approach is that he sees pluralism merely as an empirical fact. He fails to see that it might also be a value. If we eschew conceiving of pluralism largely as a danger to the stability of institutions and persons, we can also see it as an opportunity. But if pluralism entails opportunities, it can itself become a value; overcoming pluralism or returning to a pre-pluralistic state is then no longer desirable. Think of values like toleration and religious freedom as relating not to my own faith but to that of others: I want them to have the opportunity to develop their own authentic and unforced relationship to God. Such a value is certainly not based on a weaker conviction than intolerant attitudes, as if tolerance were merely the passive acceptance of others for want of realistic and preferable alternatives, such as their enforced conversion, liquidation, or expulsion. Tolerance can be an intensely held conviction that motivates people to struggle against the enemies of tolerance.

Isaiah Berlin's philosophy of value pluralism goes even further.[8] For him, values are irreducibly different, such that they can never be fully synthesized into a homogeneous value system. The dream of establishing a single value system would then always risk degenerating into a totalitarian project. This version of value pluralism leads to a tragic view of history, because it recognizes that progress always also means loss. Here, the idea of conflict between value systems loses much of its plausibility: We are confronted not with hermetically sealed alternatives, but rather we are able to relate value systems to experiences from which they emerged and which they make meaningful. And such experiences do not remain foreign to us; though it requires some effort, we can in principle translate them into our own "language." Berger's evocation of supposedly premodern institutions and value systems, which are bounded and taken for granted, fails to help us understand the specificities of the present.

Within the context of debates on Berger's work in the United States itself, several authors have pointed to the fact that no religious community has ever enjoyed a complete territorial monopoly in that country; neither has this been the case in Europe in any total sense, as we have just seen. Those who assume that such a monopoly once existed tend to overstate the traumas of adaptation experienced by religious communities as a consequence of modern pluralism. "Only very few of the hundreds of religious organizations thriving in the U.S. today, probably only the Episcopal Church, had to adapt to the pluralistic situation. Most of them were born into it."[9] The long tradition of religious pluralism in the United States has now birthed an entire sociological school, a "new paradigm for the sociological study of religion" that practically reverses Berger's assumption. This view not only rejects the idea that religious pluralism weakens religious convictions but suggests that it, in fact, explains the enduring religious vitality of the United States.

Let us now consider these *sociological* arguments more closely. As mentioned previously, they have been developed mostly in the United States, using that country as an empirical basis. Crucial to these arguments is the historical fact that this religious vitality is not, as it might seem at first, a result of the Puritan heritage, because it intensified over the course of the nineteenth and early twentieth centuries. It is therefore wrong to view secularization as a necessary corollary of modernization and to suggest that the United States is merely lagging behind Europe. On this view, religious vitality is in fact anchored in the constitutional separation of state and church in the United States in the late eighteenth century, and thus in the organic pluralism of religious communities, which compete in a "market" to satisfy people's "demand" for religion. In this situation, religious communities are economically dependent on financial support from their "customers" (rather than the state). This makes an entrepreneurial attitude on the part of the churches and religious communities more probable, opens up opportunities for the founders of new religious enterprises, engenders internal flexibility within religious organizations, and encourages religious groups to play an active role in the mobilization of certain interests, such as those of immigrant ethnic groups. If a society is becoming increasingly individualized, religious groups of the U.S. type are particularly capable of adapting to this. And although these assumptions apply in the main to Protestant communities, whose theological differences have lost much of their importance (while political differences have gained in importance), this Protestant sphere influences all the other religious communities as well. "In America even the Catholics are Protestants," as G. K. Chesterton remarked almost a century ago.

Most of these arguments have been developed by rational-choice sociologists.[10] Their work is subject to intense debate, though most authors, including nonrational choicers, accept that religious pluralism and religious vitality are linked,[11] with the exception of a small number of scholars who claim that all evidence of such a connection is based on mathematical errors[12] in measuring these two dimensions.

But Europe is a more difficult case. Some European countries feature a high level of religious activity despite being dominated by one religious community (Catholicism in Poland and Ireland). In other regions, such as Scandinavia, the abolition of the state church might even have strengthened secularization. The link cannot be quite as simple as radical "economists of religion" assume. If a geographically highly concentrated religious group experiences itself as a minority in a wider context, it can obviously remain vital despite its territorial monopoly. The process involved when an individual switches from one religious community to another is not as arbitrary as the economic model alleges. The vast majority of U.S. Protestants who join other religious communities remain within the Protestant sector ("church shopping"). Other "conversions" are collective phenomena, such as the conversion of poor blacks to Islam or the attraction of Pentecostalism for Catholic immigrants from Latin America. These observations and relevant studies suggest that we should avoid generalizing the notion that "pluralism leads to religious vitality" with undue haste; we should thus be equally cautious about advising Europeans to fully disestablish their churches in order to revitalize religion. The case of East Germany requires a further correction of this model.[13] The cessation of communist religious repression did not lead to religious revival there, probably because of a real decline in religious demand. Convinced atheists do not become religiously active even if there is complete religious freedom. This means that religious demand should be considered as flexible as religious supply. The East German case must then be explained as the result of an interplay between the churches' low degree of attractiveness, which, incidentally, dates back to precommunist times, and a decline in demand that is new and unexpected. It is unexpected because even the most radical theoreticians of secularization assumed that although religion would disappear, an equivalent of some kind would arise, such as belief in the nation or human rights (Durkheim) or democracy (Dewey).

My intention in making these remarks is not simply to slightly modify and render more robust the hypothesis of a positive causal connection between pluralism and religious vitality. I wish also to point out that it is not simply the existence of an unregulated market in religion that explains its vitality in the United States. The economists of religion are as wrong in this respect as are all economists who ascribe all sorts of positive effects to unregulated markets as such. It is well known that unregulated markets normally lead to monopolies, and Randall Collins has pointed out that this is also true in the field of religion.[14] The crucial point is that this did not happen in the United States. But this is due not simply to the existence of pluralism but to the institutionalization of the value of pluralism. In the United States, religious pluralism, like religion in general, is a value that is undergirded culturally and institutionally in a number of ways. The economists of religion ignore this because of the fundamental limitations of their approach.

Although Berger and the rational choice authors are at opposite poles regarding the causal connection between religious pluralism and religious vitality, both assume that faith is somehow based on acts of choice. Again, I have serious doubts, this time of a philosophical and psychological nature, about this assumption. The assumption that people are ceaselessly calculating utility will certainly not produce a valid psychology of motivation. Decisions such as which religious community one should join might be based in part on such calculations, as one considers the various affinities or advantages involved, but it is phenomenologically inadequate to classify the actual experience constitutive of religious faith as a "choice." Religious faith is based either on traditions internalized in the process of self-formation—or on experiences of self-transcendence.[15] These experiences are characterized by a certain passivity; one is deeply moved or seized by something, one experiences self-surrender (William James). Such experiences undoubtedly require interpretation. We only know after such an experience that we have experienced something; our certainty does not extend to the interpretation of this experience, as if the former merely emanated from the latter or existed preformed in our religious and cultural interpretive patterns. We reinterpret traditions, establish new connections, come up with new, creative articulations, perhaps even religious innovations.[16] The sociological study of conversion is rich in examples of what I have in mind here. Every conversion or religious innovation certainly features a moment of decision, a point of no return, after which the old conceptual framework is reinterpreted in terms of a new one; I do not wish to deny that at such moments an act of will is necessary, a leap of faith, a willingness to follow.[17] But this will is a willingness to surrender one's self and is thus clearly distinguishable conceptually from a rational choice between preferences. Values are not long-term preferences or preferences of a higher order but reflexive standards by which we evaluate our preferences, emotionally laden ideas of the desirable rather than desires as such. They are based on a sense of what is evident and certain, which guides us in our attempts at articulation and maintains its intensity even when we become aware of the contingency of our biographies and experiences. Just as the mere knowledge of a value or acquaintance with a person produces no commitment, the mere knowledge of, or encounter with, alternatives does not shake or unsettle our existing commitments.

Berger's thesis that pluralism leads to a loss of intensity in our commitments is a result of his acceptance of the economic notion of preference. We find ourselves in an ironic situation: Berger seems to have drawn the wrong conclusion from the empirical refutation of secularization theory. He defends the old assumption of a weakening

effect of pluralism, but moves closer to the idea of religious preferences. In fact, he should have accepted the finding that pluralism can
increase religious vitality, but made it clear that this empirically valid
statement cannot be incorporated into an economistic framework
that fails to assign a central place to "value."

At this point, Berger even contradicts himself: He has, after
all, described very ably how experiences of transcendence can lay the
foundations for faith. But no sooner has he provided us with these
impressive accounts than he repeats his claim that religious convictions today are more superficial than in the past and that people with
unshakable convictions are inclined toward such robust instruments of
persuasion as "the sword, the torture chamber, and the stake" (180). I
also find quite implausible Berger's conclusion regarding morality. He
asserts that "while the pluralistic situation plunges both religion and
morality into a crisis of relativization, for most of us the possibility
of achieving some moral certainties is greater than that of achieving
religious certainty" (201). But Berger seems to confuse subjective
certainty with intersubjective plausibility. It is easier for us to reach
agreement on moral issues with people of different religious convictions, but this does not mean that we are more certain about moral
than religious matters. The believer will also respect moral commandments whose meaning might not necessarily be obvious outside of
the faith. I bring these remarks on "contingent certainty," a certainty
felt in full awareness of its contingent foundations, to a close here;
my aim here was simply to demonstrate that Berger's understanding
of faith is not fully adequate.

We have now assembled all the components necessary to formulate an alternative to Berger. Pluralism does not weaken faith but can,
under specific conditions, strengthen it. My own approach is based
on a reorientation, a shift away from pluralism and social integration
toward increasing contingency and the associated problems.[18] We call
"contingent" that which is neither necessary nor impossible; what is,
but does not have to be. *Contingent* is the counter-concept of *necessary.*
Its precise meaning thus depends on the meaning of *necessity.* The term
refers to whatever life throws at us, both the good and the terrible. But
it also covers the experience of our own freedom of decision and action
and its consequences. We speak of increasing contingency, because
our options for action, and also the number of events that result from
human action and are dependent on it, have increased. What does
this development mean for religion today? We are by now familiar

with Berger's pessimistic views on this. One reason for their seeming plausibility, particularly in Protestant circles, undoubtedly lies in the Protestant tradition's strangely ambivalent relationship to the constitutive role of institutions and of social life itself in the development of individuality. Berger's vacillation between excessively strong institutions and unbound individualism chimes perfectly with this ambivalence. This ambivalence might be productive if it leads to a search for religious organizations that encourage and enable individualization. It could become sterile if it leads to skepticism about the core of institutionalization, the practice of ritual, the language of sacredness. Robert Bellah, another great sociologist of religion, considers the Protestant anti-institutionalist bias a "flaw in the Protestant code."[19] From the vantage point of an individualist-communitarian synthesis of this kind, we can even shed new light on the history of the Reformation and Counter-Reformation. It also enables us to see more clearly the constructive potential that increasing contingency entails. As is evident at the level of personal relationships, it is certainly possible to develop new forms adapted to increased contingency. "From institution to companionship": This was the phrase deployed within U.S. sociology of the family in the inter-war period. And this was, of course, also intended to counter the notion that the only alternative to rigid institutions was loss of direction and behavioral insecurity. However, the effort involved in defining and coordinating relationships increases, as does the functional necessity for a sensitive awareness of the other and of the specific aspects of different situations. But this in itself brings benefits and at least the prospect of a new type of stability.

Much the same can be said of faith and morality. In other places, I have distinguished among three respects in which value commitments must adapt in order to match the conditions of increasing contingency. These are (1) proceduralization, (2) value generalization, and (3) empathy. We have already come across "proceduralization" within the present context inasmuch as it refers to the recognition, valuable in itself, of profound differences in worldview and interests and restricting oneself to the peaceful resolution of conflicts in line with rules respected by both sides. My examples of an ethos of tolerance and legally guaranteed freedom of religion refer to value articulations of precisely this type, commensurate with contingency. Through these, difference as such is no longer a reason for conflict; the rules of procedure themselves become charged with great moral significance. The trend toward proceduralization is crucial to law and morality, but not to belief in a narrower sense. This is because proceduralization has no bearing on value commitments as such, insofar as individuals are prepared only to agree to common procedures in dealing with one another, whatever their value commitments might be.

In the case of the second respect, value generalization, this looks quite different.[20] Here, as different, specific value traditions attempt to come to terms with one another, they develop a general, in the main, more abstract understanding of what they have in common. Thus, in dialogue with one another, every world religion can, for example, develop its own potential to justify human rights and the idea of universal human dignity. Of course, this works only if no religious tradition expects another to abandon its right to exist and if there is no expectation that all religious traditions should take second place to rationalist justifications. Rather, in value generalization, the affective backing of a religious tradition, its particular binding power, is retained.

Third, increased contingency calls for the development of empathic faculties. It constantly confronts individuals with situations in which they themselves have to find out what they wish to do, ought to do, and are able to do. And this they can do only by empathizing with the unique circumstances of their partners in action and action situations. An element of increased freedom thus enters into the attachment to people, values, and religious communities; attachment depends on the individual's free consent, which must be periodically reconfirmed, to a greater degree than in the past.

Of the three forms of value orientation commensurate with contingency mentioned here, value generalization seems to me the most important. This is because proceduralization and empathy remain devoid of content unless they emerge from value generalization. Although some people undoubtedly have a greater capacity for empathy than others, we also know that the extent to which people are in fact willing to have moral feelings toward others, thus allowing their capacities to find expression, also depends on motivations fueled by substantial values, such as brotherly love. And the process by which legal or participatory procedures become second nature always risks regressing to the mere calculation of self-interest if there are no values motivating one to perceive these procedures as valuable in themselves. Thus, in my opinion, the imparting of values must also dominate efforts to inculcate empathy and training in procedures.

In light of these reflections, how should those called to communicate values and faith best approach their work? It is certainly essential that they emerge from the self-intimidation anchored in secularization theory. This has turned into nothing less than a self-fulfilling prophecy in Europe; anyone who believes in it becomes mired in a kind of antimodern obstinacy, as if he were clinging to his faith in opposition to the tendencies of modernization, but is more or less aware that he is fighting a losing battle. This leads people to systematically assess too pessimistically the prospects of processes of individualization in the sphere of faith. On one level, this relates to the conception of history and society embedded in the churches' self-image. The second level comes into focus if we recall my basic idea that the origin of values lies in experiences, and that faith is an interpretation of experiences of self-transcendence. If this is correct, the education system can impart values only to the extent that it permits and encourages experiences constitutive of values or helps people maieutically to articulate and interpret such experiences. Third, every process of this kind necessarily entails a personal dimension. In the absence of personal testimony, lessons on values communicate indifference; but the representation of values by individuals requires that they be willing to empathize, proceduralize, and generalize values. Fourth, we must bear in mind that educational processes can be subjected to intentional control only to a very limited degree; on the other hand, they take place ceaselessly. This means that the character of the educational institutions themselves, their architectural state, their internal structures, and their self-image as a way of life or their lack of such a self-image often have a greater impact on the processes of education than the intentions of those responsible. Happily, religious institutions of education in Germany have always been more aware of this than their state counterparts. Fifth and finally, it is impossible to impart values if one fails to articulate them in keeping with the times. Thus, every effort we make to impart values and every reflection on our educational tasks must be imbued with a modicum of doubt as to whether we ourselves credibly embody the values we promulgate.

NOTES

1. Peter L. Berger, *A Far Glory: The Quest for Faith in an Age of Credulity* (New York: Free Press, 1994); subsequent page references in the text refer to this book.

2. José Casanova, *Public Religions in the Modern World* (Chicago: University of Chicago Press, 1994).

3. Peter L. Berger, "Protestantism and the Quest for Certainty," *The Christian Century,* August 26–September 2 (1998): 782–796.

4. Peter L. Berger, ed., *The Desecularization of the World: Resurgent Religion and World Politics* (Washington, DC: Eerdmans, 1999).

5. Hans G. Kippenberg and Kocku von Stuckrad, *Einführung in die Religionswissenschaft* (Munich: Beck, 2003), 132; another helpful text is Kippenberg and von Stuckrad, "Religionswissenschaftliche Überlegungen zum religiösen Pluralismus in Deutschland. Eine Öffnung der Perspektiven," in *Multireligiosität im vereinten Europa,* ed. Hartmut Lehmann (Göttingen: Wallstein, 2003), 145–162.

6. Arnold Gehlen, *Urmensch und Spätkultur* (Bonn: Athenäum, 1956).

7. Helmut Schelsky, "Ist die Dauerreflexion institutionalisierbar?" *Zeitschrift für evangelische Ethik* 1 (1957): 153–175.

8. Isaiah Berlin, *Four Essays on Liberty* (Oxford: Oxford University Press, 1969); Hans Joas, "Value Pluralism and Moral Universalism," in Yehuda Elkana et al., eds., *Unraveling Ties: From Social Cohesion to New Practices of Connectedness* (Frankfurt and New York: Campus, 2002), 273–283.

9. R. Stephen Warner, "Work in Progress toward a New Paradigm for the Sociological Study of Religion in the United States," *American Journal of Sociology* 98 (1993): 1044–1093, esp. 1054.

10. The best-known exponents of a rational choice approach in the sociology of religion are Roger Finke and Rodney Stark. R. Stephen Warner, mentioned in fn. 9, a key figure in the definition of a new paradigm, cannot be considered a representative of this approach. The following anthology provides a useful overview: Lawrence A. Young, ed., *Rational Choice Theory and Religion: Summary and Assessment* (New York: Routledge, 1997).

11. Such as David Voas, Daniel Olson, and Alasdair Crockett, "Religious Pluralism and Participation: Why Previous Research Is Wrong," *American Sociological Review* 67 (2002): 212–230.

12. See the following highly critical literature review: Mark Chaves and Philip S. Gorski, "Religious Pluralism and Religious Participation," *Annual Review of Sociology* 27 (2001): 261–281.

13. Wolfgang Jagodzinski, "Stagnation in den Neuen Bundesländern? Fehlt das Angebot oder fehlt die Nachfrage?" in Detlef Pollack and Gerd Pickel, eds., *Religiöser und kirchlicher Wandel in Ostdeutschland 1989–1999* (Opladen: Leske & Budrich, 2000), 48–69.

14. Randall Collins, "Stark and Bainbridge, Durkheim and Weber: Theoretical Comparisons," in Lawrence A. Young, ed., *Rational Choice Theory,* 161–180.

15. Hans Joas, *The Genesis of Values* (Chicago: University of Chicago Press, 2000). Originally published as *Die Entstehung der Werte* (Frankfurt am Main: Suhrkamp, 1997).

16. Hans Joas, "On the Articulation of Experience," in this volume.

17. William James, *The Varieties of Religious Experience* (Cambridge, MA: Harvard University Press, 1985; originally published in 1902).

18. On what follows, see Hans Joas, "Morality in an Age of Contigency," *Acta sociologica* 47 (2004): 392–399.

19. Robert Bellah, "Flaws in the Protestant Code: Some Religious Sources of America's Troubles," *Ethical Perspectives* 7 (2000): 288–299.

20. I borrow this term from the work of Talcott Parsons; see his essay "Comparative Studies and Evolutionary Change," in *Social Systems and the Evolution of Action Theory* (New York: Free Press, 1977), 279–320, esp. 307ff.

3

On the Articulation
of Experience

"The Sayable and the Unsayable" ("Le dicible et l'indicible") is the title of one of the most beautiful and widely read texts written by Cornelius Castoriadis.[1] The essay is a homage to and a meditation on the philosophy of Maurice Merleau-Ponty, particularly his late attempts to develop a phenomenology of language after writing the "Phenomenology of Perception" and then to get beyond phenomenology by means of a philosophy of language; the title of the essay is itself a variation on Merleau-Ponty's book title *Le visible et l'invisible*.[2] My meditation on Castoriadis's meditation has a double purpose. It should allow me to situate one important feature of Castoriadis's thinking in the history of twentieth-century philosophy, and it should help to find out how exactly Castoriadis's ideas are related to current attempts at revitalizing pragmatism in social theory. My main question is: How is Castoriadis's post-phenomenological conception of language related to the "linguistic turn" in twentieth-century philosophy? Is the emphasis on creativity and the imaginary burdened from the beginning with an inadequate understanding of language—or is Castoriadis's philosophy able to offer us some guidance in the attempts to preserve the achievements of the linguistic turn, while also going beyond the dominant ways of thinking about language in the analytical tradition?

This question is a pressing one, because we can find traces of the understanding that Castoriadis's philosophy is "pre-linguistic" or insufficiently intersubjectivist even in the writings of sympathetic critics—like Jürgen Habermas when he criticizes the notion of a "monadic core" of the psyche as "an inadequate mediation of individual and society,"[3] or in Axel Honneth when he associates Castoriadis with Henri Bergson and suspects an ontological salvation of the revolutionary ideal as the main thrust of Castoriadis's thinking.[4]

But the question gets even more pressing when we observe that there is a direct parallel to it in the current debates about the pragmatist understanding of experience and creativity. For analytic philosophers Quine, Sellars (and Davidson) have definitively destroyed the two (or three) so-called dogmas of empiricism and demonstrated that we can never hope to test basic individual propositions one by one against experience; our experience is, according to them, always already mediated through prior understanding so that we can never reach unschematized, nonlinguistic "pure experience." And this is often taken as a refutation of the pragmatist understanding of experience as well. Even Richard Rorty, who has in many respects become one of the sharpest critics of the analytical tradition and one of the main proponents of the revitalization of pragmatism, has remained orthodox in this respect and considers the notion of experience in James and Dewey as that part of the pragmatist heritage we should waive.[5] So let us see whether the idea that there is a necessary tension between the sayable and the unsayable is indeed obsolete and naive, or whether this idea—what I call "the problem of articulation"—can lead us any farther.

Right at the beginning of his essay, Castoriadis makes clear that he sees Merleau-Ponty's unfinished attempts to write about language[6] as the superior alternative to the two other versions of a "linguistic turn" prevalent in the middle of the twentieth century.

> Antedating by many years the linguistic epidemic, this movement of Merleau-Ponty's has nothing in common with the universal extrapolation of a simplistic pseudo-model of language to which we have latterly been treated, any more than with a "linguistic philosophy" claiming to provide a solution to all questions through the elucidation and definition of permitted word usage. (120)

Obviously, Castoriadis cannot bring himself to even pronounce the name of structuralism here, and he speaks about the Wittgensteinian tradition mostly as a reductionist and deluded form of philosophy. But Merleau-Ponty can be the superior *alternative* for him exactly because he moved in the same direction as the other philosophers of language, though in a more complex way. The direction in which Merleau-Ponty was moving is the overcoming of the philosophy of consciousness, of a philosophy that assumes that there is an immaterial entity or sphere called consciousness and that there is a relationship between this consciousness and the world that becomes only secondarily translated into language. But such an understanding of consciousness proves to be untenable as soon as we take language seriously: "[T]he acquisition of language is the precondition of thought. Thus there is no *Sinngebung* by means of which the subject confers meaning upon signs that are devoid of it" (121). It becomes clear at the outset that Castoriadis certainly does not defend a "pre-linguistic turn" position here. He emphasizes how much Merleau-Ponty had to struggle with Husserl's philosophy and the primacy of perception in the epistemological and ontological heritage, and he is well aware that Merleau-Ponty's endeavors had not reached their goal when Merleau-Ponty's life ended. In a later essay, "Merleau-Ponty et le poids de l'héritage ontologique," and in the preface to "La découverte de l'imagination,"[7] Castoriadis specifies further why he thinks Merleau-Ponty's lack of success is not just owing to his premature death but also to immanent problems in his thinking. For Castoriadis, Merleau-Ponty's fusion of language and thinking is not sufficient, because this makes the chasm between perception and language even wider; he tries to grasp an imaginary that lies below perception, thinking, and language. For present purposes, it is sufficient to point out that Castoriadis obviously wants to go farther than Merleau-Ponty ever did in the overcoming of the philosophy of consciousness. We do not know yet how far Castoriadis himself was successful, but these first pages of the essay are at least an indication that Castoriadis certainly did not propose to go back behind the "linguistic turn" but proposed a specific version of it.

Why did he have to look for a specific version of the "linguistic turn" and could not be content with what the structuralists, Wittgenstein, or Peirce and Mead had to offer? Castoriadis is again very clear in his objections as far as structuralism is concerned. For him, structuralism is not the overcoming of phenomenology in particular and the philosophy of consciousness in general, but its reverse, the other side of the coin.

> The inseparability of thinking and speaking has clearly two sides to it, and to say that there is no pure thought is equally to say that there are no pure signs. The philosophy of a sovereign constituting

consciousness which only considers disincorporated noemata that are able to present themselves in person derives from the same illusion as does a structuralist or semiotic ideology, which takes account only of collections of arbitrary characteristics from which a combinatory would extract some will-o'-the-wisp meaning. (122)

Castoriadis denies that linguistic theory has indeed shown meaning to be nothing but a combination of signs, merely the difference between the bearers of meaning. Though it is true that the relation between the signified and the signifier is not an empirical or logical one, what is decisive is that the relation of a sign to a meaning is the result of the institutionalization of a sign system, and that sign systems must be understood together with their extra-systemic references to what is perceived and intended. The arbitrary character of the sign, to which structuralism attaches such importance, is thus retained, but it is accounted for by a process of institutionalization. In this way, Castoriadis reveals the meaning-originating accomplishments of the subject, behind structuralism's back, as it were.

In his essay, Castoriadis explains at length that although the signs are arbitrary, the organization of the world is not. This does not lead him back to a conception of language and perception as the copying of an objective world—of course not; but it keeps him away again from the mere reversal of such a copy theory, namely, the assumption of an arbitrary organization of the world. "The false logic of either/or here again has no purchase, for it can conceive of language (and likewise thought) only in terms of the dilemma between a description that mirrors a world in itself and a wholly arbitrary organization—both of which are equally impossible, equally meaningless formulations" (123). The world plays its role in the processes of institutionalization and actualization of sign systems.

Unfortunately, we cannot find a similarly elaborate argument in Castoriadis's writings about Wittgenstein on the one hand or Peirce and Mead on the other. This is particularly deplorable, because the pragmatist understanding of signs also has this threefold character.[8] But what we can find is a clear specification of the problem Castoriadis demands to be solved in the framework of a philosophy of language. His question is how the new can come into the framework of a linguistically constituted universe. This universe must not become hermetically sealed. Do we have to assume that, if all our experiences are based on linguistic schemes, there can be no new experiences in the world, only recombinations of existing elements? Wouldn't that repeat the errors of an older rationalism for which the perceptual flux is nothing but "a phenomenal illusion, resulting from the unceasing recombination in new forms of mixture, of unalterable elements, coeval with the world. These elements are supposed to be the only real beings; and, for the intellect once grasped by the vision of them there can be nothing genuinely new under the sun."[9] To put it in Habermasian language: Where do the new validity claims come from—before they become the subject matter of a rationalizing discourse? Are they just mutations coming up at random or in a purely irrational sphere so that their genesis is completely irrelevant for the justification of their validity?

At this point of their reflections about the role of experience, both Merleau-Ponty and Castoriadis refer to an experience that is familiar to everybody. It is the experience of a gap, "a void which swells in the already expressed; a void which is determined in the sense that the one who is about to speak knows that there is something other and more to be said than what has already been said, but knows nothing positive beyond that fact, beyond the fact that it is not said by what has already been said" (132). And a few pages later: "[I]t is true that thought in *statu nascendi* knows full well what it does not want to say, what it is not to be confused with; or that it has no problem in saying of any hazarded formulation: no, that is not what I meant. But this is a virtuality kept in reserve, which is only mobilised accidentally and partially" (134). Again, there is a surprising parallel in the writings of William James, who describes a similar experience, not in the context of one's taking part in a discussion but in the process of writing:

> As I now write, I am in one of these activity situations. I "strive" after words, which I only half prefigure, but which, when they shall have come, must satisfactorily complete the nascent sense I have of what they ought to be. The words are to run out of my pen, which I find that my hand actuates so obediently to desire that I am hardly conscious either of resistance or of effort. Some of the words come wrong, and then I do feel a resistance, not muscular but mental, which instigates a new installment of my activity, accompanied by more or less feeling of exertion.[10]

In both these descriptions, the idea of "expression" in the sense of a pre-linguistically constituted meaning that only secondarily becomes translated into language is clearly overcome; but it is not replaced by the image of a closed set of linguistic meanings forming a finite repertory for the possibilities of experience. Merleau-Ponty and Castoriadis as well as James take our experiences of articulation seriously. They see the meaning available to us as the sedimentation of earlier attempts at articulation, and they see articulation not as the task of a few geniuses but as an everyday problem for every human being, so that Castoriadis can write: "The very possibility of that rich and condensed creation which constitutes new expression is dependent upon the anonymous, daily creation in which everyone participates and whereby, through constant transformation, the vitality of language is preserved" (138).

Castoriadis's intention has now become unambiguous. He fully accepts the linguistic turn, but he wants to secure the possibility of novelty and creation against the view of a linguistically closed universe. Therefore, the investigation of our experience of articulation, of the tension between what has already been said and what has to be said, becomes crucial. But this insight leads to three somewhat paradoxical conclusions that are only partly recognized by Castoriadis.

First, if it is true that articulation arises out of a gap or a void, then it seems to follow that we become aware of our experiences mostly when it is difficult to articulate them. That is at least how I understand Castoriadis's sentence: "It is through this process of fixing meaning—without which it would be unable to function—that language makes possible the nonfixable, without which it would not be language" (133).

This conclusion can be called "somewhat paradoxical" because it might look like that, at least as long as we think about experiences in the framework of a philosophy of consciousness. In that framework, we would have to assume that we have experiences all the time, but that only a few of them undergo the process of translation from the pre-linguistic to the linguistic. In Castoriadis's framework, however, we should not talk of experiences as long as we don't feel the need to articulate something new. When everything goes smoothly and there is no tension between our feelings and the patterns of culture or the conversation around us, we would not be justified to speak of an experience. This, of course, is the deeply pragmatist idea that a feeling of activity arises out of resistance, the idea of causality out of practical effort—and this was, incidentally, exactly the context in which James presented his phenomenological description of "writing."

But one could say that Castoriadis puts the insight better even than the pragmatists, more consistently oriented to language than at least James, because he says that it is language that institutes a framework that allows us to articulate the experience that we find an articulation inadequate. Without language, it would be impossible to articulate the limits of our linguistic abilities to articulate. We would not even become aware of them. Thus, Castoriadis sees that there is not simply a tension between available language and intentions to speak, but that this tension itself can be articulated in language and becomes an experience only because it can be articulated. Merleau-Ponty had already asserted: "The reason why the thematization of the signified does not precede speech is that it is the result of it."[11]

Second, Castoriadis is fully aware of the next consequence, namely, that if we see meaning as the result of articulation, we also have to see meaning as dead without rearticulation. Understanding or reception thus become rearticulation. He writes: "A new music, states Merleau-Ponty, itself ultimately creates its own public, and we can also say that a public creates itself as a public for this new music. Still, these two movements are not superimposable. There is a fundamental asymmetry" (137). He emphasizes this asymmetry of the two processes, but leaves no doubt that both are of a fundamentally creative character. Without rearticulation, the articulation remains dead. In the words of Paul Valéry, one could say that "poetry on paper has no existence whatsoever. It is like an appliance in the closet, like a stuffed animal on the shelf."[12] And Castoriadis also knows that such rearticulation is a continual, ongoing process. But in his meditations, there is no place for another implication of this thought that had a prominent place in William James's thinking about novelty: that the process can also start at the other end, so to speak, that we can encounter an articulation that suddenly makes us aware of an experience we once had. This encounter can be accompanied by feelings of enthusiasm and is certainly familiar to everybody who loves, for example, reading. It is probably even a reason why reading can become such an addiction. It does not make sense here to assume that we had constantly felt the need for a particular articulation, but—being unable to find the right words—decided to wait for years until we finally could find them in a book. It makes more sense to conceive of the process of articulation here as a process that can take place in two directions, from percepts to concepts or from concepts to percepts, as William James would have put it. In

this sense, a language and a culture offer us rich possibilities for articulation that go far beyond our needs for articulation so that they
structure this need and can even lead us astray to the point where we
falsely convince ourselves that we are having a particular experience
(Madame Bovary!). The problem of articulation thus proves to be
a specific case of what I have called—in my book on *The Creativity
of Action*—"a non-teleological interpretation of the intentionality of
action." Castoriadis understood that action in general is not simply
the interplay of values and impulses but is characterized by the
creative concretization of values as well as the constructive satisfac-
tion of impulses.[13] But he might not have emphasized sufficiently
the role cultural patterns play in these processes of articulation and
creative action.

There is a third consequence of Castoriadis's view on
articulation—a consequence clearly seen, but only partly elaborated
by him. If we are really talking about the articulation of new meanings
and not about a mere recombination of given significations, a return
to the emergence of the new becomes necessary. Castoriadis asks:

> But why is it that this meaning, which is in principle also visible
> from where we are, arises elsewhere, and only elsewhere, and only
> in a time that must be rediscovered? Why is it that for all its ideality
> we are not spared the long visit to its place of origin, the years in
> residence there, and even, perhaps, our forgetting ourselves there
> if we really desire to see? (131)

We should not understand this return to the emergence in a strictly
chronological sense, though it may have such a dimension. It is rather
a return to the subjectivity of the articulation. One finds confirmation
for this interpretation in the passage in which Castoriadis writes:

> The instituting origin is therefore not simply that of an *Urstiftung*
> upon which language, culture, a definitive set of institutions have
> arisen once and for all. Nor is it simply that of a *Stiftung* of succes-
> sive and succeeded languages and cultures. The instituting origin is
> always there, upright, "vertically" transversing, as it is put in "The
> Visible and the Invisible," the here and now. And if it is there, this
> is because the subject is origin. The subject, and subjects. For this
> ever-immanent origin privileges certain sites at various times, but
> excludes none. (138)

Merleau-Ponty and Castoriadis try to grasp the suffering and the silence preceding the articulation of the new—and "the final moment of its triumphant realization in a phrase or theme or gesture finally found" (137). Castoriadis is eager to distinguish the intensity of such "silent thought" from "ecstasy or stupid 'intuition'" (141)—a move again intended to distinguish his thinking and that of Merleau-Ponty from Bergson on the one hand and presumably Bataille on the other. But he is perhaps too quick in his dismissal here. Though he is right to distance himself from the ideas of a nonsymbolic intuition and an ecstatic disappearance of all subjectivity, it would be more appropriate to try to reformulate, on the basis of his understanding of articulation, the experiences of intuitive certainty and ecstatic fusion. In the thinking of Merleau-Ponty, his constant relationship to the art of painting counterbalanced his views on linguistic articulation, making clear the limits of language in a very fundamental way by referring to aesthetic experiences in a nonlinguistic art. In the thinking of William James, a similar counterbalance comes from his openness toward religious, particularly mystical experiences, which are never adequately communicable. I cannot find a comparable openness toward aesthetic and certainly not toward religious experience in Castoriadis. Perhaps the experience of psychoanalytic therapy occupies the place in his philosophy that art or religion had in Merleau-Ponty or James. What is common to all three of them, and what has to be a necessary part of our understanding of communication, is that in all these cases *subjective* experience is communicated without becoming *objective*—is communicated in ways that retain its subjective character.[14]

I would go even further and claim that all communication about our commitments and attachments—to other people and to values—is of this character and hence cannot take on and should not take on the character of a rationalized discourse. This does not imply that such a rationalized discourse should not play any role at all. It is—in my eyes—the right instance for the justification and adjudication of cognitive and normative validity claims and thus crucial for parts of epistemology and moral philosophy. But Castoriadis's philosophy of creativity, novelty, and articulation points out—like pragmatism—that there is a wider framework—a framework in which the emergence of new hypotheses, new values, new "nuclei of sense" (131) is taken into account and in which thus justification plays the role of critique, but cannot be considered to be constitutive itself.

It is not possible to spell out here all the consequences this has for moral philosophy and social theory. Let me therefore restrict myself to a few remarks about the articulation of moral feelings and its importance for historical processes of value change.[15] For this purpose, one has to start with the assumption that our "strong evaluations" (Charles Taylor) are embodied in our moral feelings, but that there can also be a gap between our moral feelings and our reflective values. Perhaps we realize with astonishment that we fail to feel guilt or outrage even though we ourselves or others have infringed upon what we took to be our values. Conversely, perhaps we are tormented by feelings of guilt or are seized by outrage even though we are under the impression that none of our consciously endorsed values has been infringed upon. The relationship between strong evaluations embodied in our moral feelings and our consciously endorsed values is therefore not without tension.

The process of articulating our moral feelings does not have a clearly determinable direction. Rather, it describes the hermeneutic circle. We move to and fro between the levels of our feelings, of our own interpretations of these feelings and the publicly established interpretations. Our present self-interpretation, despite its intersubjective constitution, is not necessarily identical with the public interpretation of an instance. Our feelings, despite their need for interpretation, are not completely absorbed into our self-interpretations. In addition to that, these three levels are all directed toward incidents, events, and situations that likewise bring their own character antagonistically into play. Something new is produced in this very interplay between the various levels. If it is difficult or impossible to express one's own feelings in the vocabulary available in a given culture, then innovative forms can perhaps be invented or can be borrowed from other cultures.

Thus, we should not simply speak of an interplay between experiences and articulation but rather of an interplay among the situation experienced, our pre-reflective experience, our individual articulation, and the cultural repertoire of interpretative patterns. We might constantly strive for an attunement between these levels, but we will only rarely and never permanently attain it. But in this very process—in the attempts to achieve this attunement—new values are produced. A sociological analysis has to combine such an understanding of the dynamics of articulation with the more conventional, one could also say, "materialist" dimensions like the resources available for the dissemination of new ideas, the processes of selection and institutionalization, the world of interests and struggles.[16] Even if one does not go into these questions at all, these remarks should be sufficient to signal a counterposition to all explanatory models starting from reductionist premises—be they Marxist, Nietzschean, or whatever.

Nobody has done more than Cornelius Castoriadis to lay bare such reductionist views in Marxism, but also in structuralism and in an existentialism of arbitrary choice. At the end of his meditations on Merleau-Ponty, he quotes from "The Visible and the Invisible": "The open, in the sense of a hole, that is Sartre, is Bergson, is negativism or ultra-positivism (Bergson)—indiscernible. There is no *nichtiges Nichts*" (144).[17] And Castoriadis adds: "It is opening, then, in the sense of the work of opening, constantly renewed inauguration, performance of the primitive spirit, the spirit of praxis. Or, in other words: the subject is that which opens" (144).

NOTES

1. Cornelius Castoriadis, "The Sayable and the Unsayable," in *Crossroads in the Labyrinth* (Cambridge, MA: MIT Press, 1984), 119–144; subsequent page references in the text refer to this book. For an overview of Castoriadis's thinking, see Hans Joas, "Institutionalization as a Creative Process," in *Pragmatism and Social Theory* (Chicago: University of Chicago Press, 1993), 154–171.

2. Maurice Merleau-Ponty, *Le visible et l'invisible* (Paris: Gallimard, 1964); trans.: *The Visible and the Invisible* (Evanston, IL: Northwestern University Press, 1968).

3. Jürgen Habermas, "Excursus on Cornelius Castoriadis: The Imaginary Institution," in *The Philosophical Discourse of Modernity* (Cambridge, MA: MIT Press, 1987), 327–335.

4. Axel Honneth, "Rescuing the Revolution with an Ontology: On Cornelius Castoriadis's Theory of Society," *Thesis Eleven* 14 (1986): 62–78.

5. This comes out very clearly in Richard Rorty, "Dewey between Hegel and Darwin," in Herman J. Saatkamp Jr., ed., *Rorty and Pragmatism: The Philosopher Responds to His Critics* (Nashville: Vanderbilt University Press, 1995), 1–15. An excellent critique of Rorty in this respect has been published by Richard Shusterman, "Dewey on Experience: Foundationalism or Reconstruction," *Philosophical Forum* 26 (1994): 127–148.

6. See, above all, Merleau-Ponty, *Signs* (Evanston, IL: Northwestern University Press, 1964).

7. Castoriadis, "Merleau-Ponty et le poids de l'héritage ontologique," *Fait et à faire. Les carrefours du labyrinthe* 5 (Paris: Seuil, 1997): 157–195 (an English translation was published in *Thesis Eleven* 36 [1993], 1–36); Castoriadis, "La

découverte de l'imagination," *Domaines de l'homme. Les carrefours du labyrinthe* 2 (Paris: Seuil, 1986), 327–363, esp. 330ff.

8. On the difference between pragmatist and structuralist semiotic theory, see Eugene Rochberg-Halton, "Situation, Structure, and the Context of Meaning," *Sociological Quarterly* 23 (1982):156–180.

9. William James, *Some Problems of Philosophy* (New York: Longmans, Green & Co., 1911), 149. For an interpretation of James's philosophy from this perspective, see William Joseph Gavin, *William James and the Reinstatement of the Vague* (Philadelphia: Temple University Press, 1992).

10. Ibid., 210f. A brilliant early expression can be found in Heinrich von Kleist (1777–1811), "Über die allmähliche Verfertigung der Gedanken beim Reden," in *Werke* (Munich: Hanser, 1966), 810–814.

11. Merleau-Ponty, *The Visible and the Invisible,* 90.

12. My translation. The original quotation is: "La poésie sur le papier n'a aucune existence. Elle est alors ce qu'est un appareil dans l'armoire, un animal empaillé sur un rayon." Paul Valéry, *Cahiers,* vol. 2 (Paris: Gallimard, 1974), 1141.

13. Hans Joas, *The Creativity of Action* (Chicago: University of Chicago Press, 1996), 148–167, here 163. I have been influenced here by Dietrich Böhler, *Rekonstruktive Pragmatik* (Frankfurt am Main: Suhrkamp, 1985), 234ff.

14. I find a very convincing analysis of this in an essay by the (late) East German writer Franz Fühmann, "Das mythische Element in der Literatur," in *Essays, Gespräche, Aufsätze 1964–1981* (Rostock: Hinstorff, 1983), 82–139.

15. For the following remarks I am clearly indebted to Charles Taylor's important thoughts on articulation in the first part of his masterful book *Sources of the Self* (Cambridge, MA: Harvard University Press, 1989), 3–107. See also Hans Joas, *The Genesis of Values* (Chicago: University of Chicago Press, 2000), 132ff.

16. For an impressive attempt to develop such an integrative framework for the sociology of cultural change, see Robert Wuthnow, *Communities of Discourse: Ideology and Social Structure in the Reformation, the Enlightenment, and European Socialism* (Cambridge, MA: Harvard University Press, 1989). Wuthnow devotes the introduction (1–22) to "The Problem of Articulation," but uses the term somewhat differently, namely, for the connection between "interpretation" and "explanation," to say it in a Weberian language, and not, as I do here, for an improved understanding of "interpretation."

17. The quotation is from Merleau-Ponty, *The Visible and the Invisible,* 196.

PART 2

Between Theology and Social Science

4

Sociology and the Sacred: Key Texts in the Sociology of Religion

The social sciences neither speak of God nor pose questions about Him, but religion was one of the key topics of interest at the time of their disciplinary emergence.[1] Those texts that inform substantially the theoretical and methodological repertoire of sociology to this day, and are thus rightly described as classics, appeared in the main between 1890 and 1920. The division into two hostile camps of those expounding the Enlightenment or materialist critique of religion on the one hand and those inclined toward its restorative functionalization on the other, typical of the late eighteenth and early nineteenth centuries, was not simply carried on by the great figures of sociology. They certainly had to position themselves within this arena. But the questions that captured their attention and determined their view of religion were new. At the present time, when Germany and large parts of Europe are witnessing a dramatic abandonment of religious traditions, the perspective provided by classical texts in the sociology and theory of religion, from time to time even against the authors' original intentions, can open up new points of access to religious phenomena—precisely because these works on religion do not speak in a language that the modern reader finds hard to understand or off-putting.

It was psychology rather than sociology that brought about a sea change in the scientific study of religion in the early twentieth century. In 1902, William James's book *The Varieties of Religious Experience*[2] appeared in the United States; it quickly came to be seen as embodying a revolutionary upheaval in the history of religious studies. Even today, it has lost none of its freshness. James's fundamental methodological idea involved making *religious experiences* the starting point of a theory of religion. With supreme one-sidedness, he proposed that we initially disregard entirely theological doctrine and religious institutions and concentrate on personal religion, that is, the solitary individual's relationship to the Divine, however understood. Of course, James was also aware that doctrines and institutions grow from the seeds of the individual experience of the Divine, but for him these always remained secondary phenomena as against the primary phenomena of individual religious experience.

By selecting this point of departure, James freed himself in one fell swoop from the intellectual straitjacket of the historicist or evolutionist religious studies of the nineteenth century as well as from attempts to interpret the religious as merely the displaced expression of other more real needs. He had in mind primarily the vulgar medical materialism of the nineteenth century, but the twentieth century was to bring forth similar far more influential theories in the shape of modern Marxism and psychoanalysis, which interpreted the religious as encouraging hopes of justice and prosperity solely in the hereafter or as the projection of a father image or the longing for erotic fusion upon imaginary phenomena.

But how can religious experiences be studied? James amassed a wealth of material in pursuit of his project. He made use, first of all, of writings, diaries, and autobiographical accounts by religious virtuosos: saints, the founders of sects, and other religious masterminds from every historical era and world religion. Second, he drew on a collection of autobiographical accounts of religious conversion by contemporary Americans. His book contains long verbatim passages from both types of account, and this is surely why it is so gripping and deeply moving for many readers, quite apart from James's own brilliance as a writer. On the basis of these texts, in chapters on conversion and prayer, mystical experience and personal "rebirth," James develops a rich phenomenology of the religious. In sharp contrast to the Victorian era when religion meant morality with emotional trimmings, James distinguishes sharply between morality and religion.

Whereas morality restricts our options for action and prohibits certain goals and means, religion enlarges our options for action. The person guided by morality is for James a top athlete in terms of discipline, whereas the life of the religious person is anchored in a passion and excitement that arise from exceptional states of mind, but that have developed into a lasting frame of mind. James analyzes the faith of the religious person not as holding something to be true in a cognitive sense, a belief that might be shaken by discursive argument, but rather as an attitude to reality underpinned by the sure sense that a greater power is present. He compares faith with the fundamental vibrancy felt by lovers: "A lover has notoriously this sense of the continuous being of his idol, even when his attention is addressed to other matters and he no longer represents her features. He cannot forget her; she uninterruptedly affects him through and through."[3] The sense of certainty and an enlightenment hard to put into words go hand in hand with a willing embrace of existence and a perception of the beauty of the world that might extend to ecstasy. James repeatedly contrasts the condition of faith with the tendency for the color to leach out of the world of those suffering melancholy and depression. What he finds particularly interesting about conversion and prayer is the nonvolitional character of the religious, the communication with the power from which the individual's life force flows. This power cannot be forced, but must graciously reveal itself to us.

For an entire generation of intellectuals, the encounter with this book was a formative experience. Traces of this encounter are evident in Heidegger and Wittgenstein, Scheler and Simmel. Among scholars of religion in Germany, Ernst Troeltsch responded most vigorously; he himself produced one of the most significant studies in the sociology of religion in 1912 in the shape of his great work *The Social Teaching of the Christian Churches* (*Die Soziallehren der christlichen Kirchen und Gruppen*),[4] whose roots lay in Protestant theology and ecclesiastical history. His study of religious groups and churches and of the everyday manifestations of Christian ethics relates these with great sophistication to the social world as a whole, "that is the State, the economic order with its division of labor, and the family."[5] James's work also came to the attention of Max Weber, presumably via Troeltsch. Weber's essay *The Protestant Ethic and the Spirit of Capitalism* appeared in 1904, certainly the most famous text in the history of the sociology of religion, if not of sociology itself. Weber's highly complex attempt to demonstrate connections between the spirit of Protestantism, particularly Calvinism and Puritanism, and the development of modern capitalism caused intense controversy the moment it appeared; this persists to this day, indicating that the author had touched not only upon an issue central to historiography but to the cultural self-image of Europe and North America. Weber himself continued to follow the thread that he had identified; he immersed himself in the study of the economic ethics of all the world religions, working through huge quantities of sources and literature in the history of religion, increasingly branching out from the comparatively narrow subject of economic ethics to the entire range of religious ideas. Even now, social scientists continue to process these uncompleted studies;[6] one of the leading contemporary sociological theorists is devoting almost his entire academic life's work to reconstructing these writings and considering them in light of the current state of knowledge.[7] Although Max Weber described himself, not without a degree of coquetry, as entirely "unmusical religiously," his writings display a fascinating capacity for understanding. But the grain of truth in his self-description was that he was always primarily interested in the *consequences* of systems of religious belief rather than those systems themselves. His writings are thus of only limited value in tackling many issues in the social scientific study of religion, despite their brilliance.

The great French sociologist Émile Durkheim goes much further than Max Weber in taking up James's idea of making religious experience central to the analysis of religion. This emphatically laicist rabbi's son never lost his interest in religious life; from the mid-1890s on, it became the center of his academic work, which culminated in the appearance of *The Elementary Forms of Religious Life* in 1912.[8] In its core empirical sections, this book presents a study of totemism, the (supposed) religion of aboriginal Australians—insofar as this was amenable to reconstruction on the basis of contemporary travelers' accounts and research reports. This choice of subject might at first sight seem off-beat and liable to put off nonspecialist readers. It is rooted in an underlying "evolutionist" assumption, namely, that we must examine the oldest forms of modern-day social phenomena in order to explain them, and that these are simpler, that is, less complex than the later forms. In the case of the origins and consequences of religious life, this meant investigating the "most primitive" form of religion still in existence. This, so it seemed, was undoubtedly totemism in Australia (and among certain Native American tribes).

Durkheim anchors his great work in a definition of religion that was to exercise a greater influence than any other within the social scientific analysis of religion: "A religion is a unified system of beliefs and practices relative to sacred things, that is to say, things set apart and surrounded by prohibitions—beliefs and practices that unite its adherents in a single moral community called a church."[9] Thus, Durkheim, like James, does not see religion exclusively as a system of belief but rather highlights the significance of ritual practices, which are more than merely the expressions of a belief. He, too, eschews defining religion in terms of a belief in God or gods or by reference to the "supernatural" (which, of course, always requires a concept of the merely natural), instead privileging the "sacred," that is, a dichotomous division of the world into the sacred and the profane. But in sharp contrast to James, for him, every aspect of the religious is social in nature; he derives all the individual's relationships to the sacred from groups or defines them as mere magic and contrasts them with the truly religious.

Durkheim identifies the idea of a force beyond the individual as the essential feature of totemism and thus the most elementary component of all religion. For him, it is not mythical figures, gods, or spirits, let alone the animals and plants, which appear to be worshipped in totemism, that ultimately underlie religious thought, but rather "vague powers, anonymous forces. These are more or less numerous, depending on the society—sometimes they are even a single force."[10] On this view, the sacredness of sacred things or practices is not rooted in their substance but is due to the fact that they are interpreted as embodying this principle of sacredness, a palpable force at work in them.

In a particularly bold move, Durkheim goes further yet, probing the origins of these notions of the power of sacredness. He reminds us that a gathering of people, especially if it exists for a fair length of time, often reduces the self-control of all those present. This could have powerful stimulating effects—inhibitions weaken and individuals' confidence increases and begins to show in their behavior. Once a certain threshold is crossed, however, this heightened sense of self is replaced by the sense of being overwhelmed, which could ultimately result in the loss of all sense of self. Durkheim has his sights set on the experience of ecstasy within the group—he talks of "collective effervescence"—and thus on the experience of loss of self, which is simultaneously the experience of a force, an extraordinary power, which carries away the individual and places him in a different world. For Durkheim himself, this force represents nothing other than the effect of the merging of individuals. But he is well aware that those affected do not in the main coolheadedly interpret the incredible experiences of loss of self, and of a force that banishes the quotidian, as a mere effect of their interaction. Such extraordinary experiences, however, cannot go uninterpreted; they urgently require integration into the everyday frame of reference, particularly once they are over and everyday life begins again. According to Durkheim, those involved achieve this by putting their experience down to preexisting powers, which they believe themselves to have come into contact with at the time and place of their gathering. Their affective certainty about the effects of higher powers, which inevitably arises from this experience of loss of self, is thus transformed into an attachment, no longer amenable to reflection, to attributes of the situation in which they had this experience. The classification of the world into two realms is anchored in this process of attribution, in accordance with whether a thing or action is associated with this extraordinary experience or not. Everything that lacks such an association is profane; everything that has it is sacred, however this may be conveyed to the individual. For Durkheim, loss of self thus entails the possibility of going beyond the bounded self toward the forces of sociality that are interpreted as sacred.

This experience, constitutive of sacredness, generates a tension in relation to everyday life. The force that arises in the extraordinary experiences carries the individual through her day. The experience of ecstasy lends the individual vitality; it revitalizes her every time it is repeated. On this basis, Durkheim addresses the origins of the concept of the soul, spirits, and God and studies the various types of rite. In so doing, he influenced research in the anthropology of religion for decades. His own point of departure, however, was a palpable concern of his day—the passionate search for a new morality capable of ensuring the social cohesion of modern society without forgoing the merits of individualism, and the search for functional equivalents of a religiosity (supposedly) withering in the modern age.

One wonders, however, whether Durkheim ever returned to contemporary French reality from his long imaginary research trip to Australia. Although contemporary questions had driven him to study the "elementary forms of religious life," his answers with respect to his time remained vague and unclear. Following his death, critics even accused Durkheim of having anticipated the collective ecstasy of fascist and national socialist mass rituals, such as the Nuremberg rallies. Such claims are unfounded. Durkheim himself in fact regarded human rights and human dignity as appropriate beliefs for modern society, but was unable to show which extraordinary experiences might generate and perpetually reinvigorate such belief. Religions, broadly conceived to take in all commitments to values or ideals, are for Durkheim something very real, phenomena sui generis that cannot be traced back to anything "ideal-free."[11]

Alongside anthropological researchers (such as Victor Turner), two very different strands of religious studies picked up Durkheim's thread. Primarily as a result of the work of the most important U.S. sociologist of the 1950s and 1960s, Talcott Parsons, Durkheim's theory of religion was read as evidence that religion has a socially integrative function. This certainly failed to do justice to the subtlety of Parsons's views,[12] but became a point of reference nonetheless. The issue of religion's socially integrative effect and its functional equivalents was put to creative use by those close to Parsons: In famous studies by Edward Shils on the coronation ceremonial of Britain's Queen Elizabeth II, for example, and particularly in the pioneering study by Robert Bellah on U.S. "civil religion"[13]—the sacralization of national symbols and the meanings contained within U.S. cultural and political tradition, deeply influenced by Christianity yet at the same time set apart from it.

The peculiar linkage of Durkheim's theory of religion with sur-realist motifs, which developed in France between the wars and found expression in the work of the so-called Collège de Sociologie, was a quite different project.[14] The most famous members of this group to explore religion are Roger Caillois and Georges Bataille. Caillois went further than the master in developing the notion of the ambivalence of the sacred and also of the profane, of which Durkheim had already taken note, the sacred being both attractive and frightening, the latter merely quotidian or wicked.[15] For him and Bataille, the experiences of the world war, violence and death, had also become intellectual challenges. Bataille searched desperately for an alternative beyond Stalinism and fascism, but was unable to see it in the traditions of the Western democracies, as he perceived them from a relatively or-thodox Marxist perspective. In his work, the dream of the proletarian revolution is fused with the project of a "heterology," which entails resisting the elimination of disorderliness and emerges as a vision of the collective, ecstatic foundation of a new anti-Christian religion as an alternative to fascism. Here, this odd development of Durkheim's work anticipates motifs of postmodern discourse.[16] Bataille examines the prospects for ecstatic sociality in the modern age and even tries, in an eccentric turn, to advance from a sociology of the sacred to a "sacred sociology": Sectarian group experiments and the living out of violent fantasies serve to bring about ecstatic experiences extolled as a route out of the ruptures of modernity.

After World War I, Rudolf Otto's slim volume *The Idea of the Holy* had an impact similar to that of James's book at the beginning of the twentieth century, initially in Germany and then worldwide.[17] Otto's roots were in Protestant theology, but he was also a widely traveled scholar of comparative religion and distinguished Indologist. In his nonacademic and energetic work, he paved the way for a synthesis of the German historicist tradition of religious studies and the phenomenology of religious experience, much of which comes from James. Although the similarity between James and Otto was noticed at an early stage,[18] to my knowledge it has never been studied systematically. Debates in Germany tended to compare him with Friedrich Schleiermacher and his definition of religion on the basis of a "sense of absolute dependency." It is at this point that Otto distances himself from Schleiermacher, for several reasons, but largely because this definition seems to him guided by a misleading subjectivism:

> According to him the religious emotion would be directly and primarily a sort of *self*-consciousness, a feeling concerning oneself in a special determined relation, viz. one's dependence. Thus, according to Schleiermacher, I can only come upon the very fact of God as the result of an inference, that is, by reasoning to a cause beyond myself to account for my "feeling of dependence." But this is entirely opposed to the psychological facts of the case. Rather, the "creature-feeling" is itself a first subjective concomitant and effect of another feeling-element, which casts it like a shadow, but which in itself indubitably has immediate and primary reference to an object outside the self.[19]

Thus, according to Otto, the phenomenology of religious experience tells us that neither the sense of self in general nor a rational conclusion that I am dependent on higher forces is constitutive of religion but rather a holistic experience of a specific quality, or the experience of an object of a specific quality. Otto's term for this quality constitutive of sacredness is *the numinous*.

For the "creature-feeling" and the sense of dependence to arise in the mind the "numen" must be experienced as present, a *numen praesens*, as in the case of Abraham. There must be felt a something "numinous," something bearing the character of a "numen," to which the mind turns spontaneously; or (which is the same thing in other words) these feelings can only arise in the mind as accompanying emotions when the category of "the numinous" is called into play.[20]

His famous book is essentially a multifaceted attempt to describe the nature of the numinous. He breaks it down into the *aweful* ("tremendum"), overpoweringness ("majestas"), energy, the wholly other ("mysterium"), as well as fascination, the monstrous, and the august. But he is interested not only in emotional qualities but also in objects' capacity to generate these feelings and in artistic and religious means of expressing the numinous. In suggestive prose, his book touches on all these motifs, without truly getting to grips with a single one of them. More than Schleiermacher, who also protested against a rationalistic theology and a morally constricted Christianity, his aim is the dialectical mediation of the rational and irrational, moral and religious. More than James and Durkheim, for whom there is no inherent relationship between the qualities of objects and their sacredness, Otto insists on a description of the numinous as a quality innate to the object itself. This is both strength and weakness: It brings to our attention a wealth of specific research topics within religious studies, but tends to diminish the significance of the power of the sacred, which potentially permeates every object of this world.

Otto's work has influenced the development of theology, religious studies, and sociology of religion in rich and intricate ways. It was continued in most consistent form in the vast life's work of the Romanian Mircea Eliade. Coming from an Indological background and initially based in Paris, he was called to Chicago through the intervention of Otto's emigrant disciple Joachim Wach. There, he founded an important school of religious studies and investigated the forms of the sacred in great detail.[21] Within the tradition of phenomenology of religion, the most important Catholic philosopher and sociologist of the first half of the twentieth century, Max Scheler, grappled intensively with Rudolf Otto. He broadly agrees with his description of the religious, but criticizes Otto's tendency to relapse to Schleiermacher's position and strives, above all, to combine an approach that focuses on religious experience with an objectivist interpretation of the subjectively experienced phenomena. For him, both Otto and James fail to grasp the fact that these "intuitions ... uncover (merely uncover, [rather than] form or construct) *ontic features of absolute holiness* which are firmly established in Christ's person and there discovered."[22] As in his philosophy of values, Scheler tends to overestimate the reach of phenomenological analyses in his theory of religion as well. For him, the subjective sense of certainty regarding values demonstrated that values objectively precede experience and are independent of it; likewise, the fact of religion becomes an indication of the existence of God. What we have here is the mirror-image of the self-assurance with which Durkheim assumed he had revealed the secret of all religions by means of sociology, just as Feuerbach, Marx, Nietzsche, and Freud claimed to have found the definitive answer. William James, meanwhile, proceeded more cautiously, tentatively, dialogically. Scheler jumps to the erroneous conclusion that James's investigation of religious experience, which asserts the existence of an intentional object of this experience, but ultimately leaves this object undefined, is merely an empirical psychology of religion, which is itself of no relevance to religion. He is unable to see that James was guided by a modest and pragmatic attitude even with respect to salvation and redemption: not the proclamation of certain knowledge of redemption but the curious and tolerant, open-minded search for it.

All the approaches to the social scientific study of religion initiated at the beginning of the twentieth century (James, Durkheim, Otto) were followed up productively over the subsequent decades. Some of these later authors (Eliade, Caillois, Parsons) have been mentioned already. The leading U.S. pragmatist, John Dewey, wrote his slim volume on religion in the tradition of James, but was also influenced by Durkheim.[23] Although his work lacks the plethora of perspectives typical of James, he introduced profound ideas on the formation of the self, the origins of ideals, and the experience of intersubjectivity and successful communication to the pragmatist theory of religion. But his aim in putting forward these ideas was the deinstitutionalization of the religious, a highly implausible development from a modern-day perspective, which he hoped would lead humanity toward faith in democracy, that is, the sacralization of democracy.

Talcott Parsons's later works went far beyond an emphasis on the socially integrative capacity of religion. Following the example of the structuralist analysis of mythologies, he began to examine the mythical core of the Judeo-Christian tradition; he believed he had found it in the form of the notion of life as a gift.[24] The leading U.S. anthropologist of religion Clifford Geertz also came from a Parsonian background; following studies of Islam in Indonesia and Morocco, he became famous largely because of his reflections on problems of anthropological methodology. His landmark essay "Religion As a Cultural System"[25] represents a step forward in social scientific theory of religion in two respects in particular. The approach to religious experiences taken by James, Durkheim, and Otto could not simply be continued following the general linguistic turn in philosophy and the social sciences, given that it was now accepted that experience is mediated through language (or symbols). Geertz's methodological reflections represent a shift away from the interpretation of experience toward the interpretation of symbols. But this shift must not lead to notions of hermetically sealed symbol systems closed to modification in light of new experiences and their articulation. Furthermore, Geertz made it clear that people typically switch back and forth constantly between religious perspectives and common sense,[26] and thus between radically different perspectives, "which are not continuous with one another but separated by cultural gaps across which Kierkegaardian leaps must be made in both directions."[27] This enables his symbolic theory of religion to avoid the risk of overestimating the cultural.

It is impossible to sum up in a few sentences the vast field of the empirical sociology of religion over the past few decades.[28] Whereas only a small number of renowned sociologists (Franz-Xaver Kaufmann, Thomas Luckmann, Joachim Matthes—and Niklas Luhmann, too, in his own way) were active in this field in Germany in the 1970s and 1980s, the vibrant religious culture of the United States has generated a great variety of important scholarly studies. The essayistic writings of Peter Berger have generally been paid most attention in Germany.[29] Key controversies currently revolve around the issues of advancing secularization and the privatization of the religious. The concept of secularization is, of course, notoriously ambiguous. Whereas in Europe the link between modernization and the decline of religion is very often treated as a matter of course, one of the central issues for scholars in the United States is whether this assumption applies at all to developments there and to what extent one may speak of a special American or, from a global perspective, of a special European path in religious terms.[30] Thomas Luckmann is the leading scholar of advancing individualization and privatization of the religious, and his work has been widely influential.[31] Although these tendencies have been important, scholars have increasingly turned their attention back to the public role of religion under conditions of individualization and differentiation. Some of the most important studies in the sociology of religion in recent years have tackled this subject.[32]

The contemporary sociology of religion requires a new synthesis on a par with the classical texts of the first half of the twentieth century. It seems to me that Robert Bellah has gone furthest in making a start on this. He has laid the foundations for such a synthesis not only in his studies on U.S. and Japanese religiosity in particular but also in theoretical works.[33] In recent writings, he further develops the symbolic theory of religion and is currently working on a sociological world history of religion. His perspective is evolutionary rather than evolutionistic. Bellah is no adherent of the myth of progress in the sphere of religion, but neither does he place all religious phenomena on the same level. By what right, for example, do we describe monotheism as religious progress? At this point, the questions posed by the sociologists of religion turn palpably into religious questions. A narrow ridge runs between religiously irrelevant sociology of religion and cryptotheology. But the social scientific study of religion requires us to travel along this very ridge. This journey might lead people to become aware of the "sacredness" in their own evaluations and worldviews and to form new relationships with the wealth of religious traditions that characterize our cultures.

NOTES

1. Some of the thinking in this chapter overlaps with that in my book *The Genesis of Values* (Chicago: University of Chicago Press, 2000). I have therefore drawn on statements made in that book in some instances.

2. William James, *The Varieties of Religious Experience* (Cambridge, MA: Harvard University Press, 1985).

3. Ibid., 66.

4. Ernst Troeltsch, *The Social Teaching of the Christian Churches*, trans. Olive Wyon (London: Allen and Unwin, 1931).

5. Ibid., 34. Troeltsch reviewed James's book (*Deutsche Literaturzeitung* 25 [1904]: esp. 3021–3027) and expressed his views in even greater detail later: Ernst Troeltsch, "Empiricism and Platonism in the Philosophy of Religion—To the Memory of William James," in *Harvard Theological Review* 5 (1912): 401–402.

6. Max Weber, *Gesammelte Aufsätze zur Religionssoziologie,* 3 vols. (Tübingen: Mohr, 1920; and numerous re-editions).

7. Wolfgang Schluchter, *Religion und Lebensführung*, 2 vols. (Frankfurt am Main: Suhrkamp, 1988).

8. Émile Durkheim, *The Elementary Forms of Religious Life* (Oxford: Oxford University Press, 2001). Originally published as *Les formes élémentaires de la vie religieuse* (Paris: Alcan, 1912).

9. Ibid., 46.

10. Ibid., 149.

11. See the last chapter of the present volume, "Human Dignity: The Religion of Modernity?"

12. Talcott Parsons, *The Structure of Social Action* (New York: McGraw Hill, 1937); Parsons, *The Social System* (New York: Free Press, 1951), esp. 367ff. For a work that clears up numerous misunderstandings, see Sigrid Brandt, *Religiöses Handeln in moderner Welt. Talcott Parsons' Religionssoziologie im Rahmen seiner allgemeinen Handlungs- und Systemtheorie* (Frankfurt am Main: Suhrkamp, 1993).

13. Edward Shils and Michael Young, "The Meaning of the Coronation" (1956), in Edward Shils, *Center and Periphery* (Chicago: University of Chicago Press, 1975), 135–152; Robert Bellah, "Civil Religion in America," in *Beyond Belief: Essays on Religion in a Post-Traditional World* (New York: Harper and Row, 1970), 168–189.

14. The most important collection is Denis Hollier, ed., *Le Collège de Sociologie 1937–39* (Paris: Gallimard, 1979).

15. Roger Caillois, *Man and the Sacred* (Glencoe, IL: Glencoe Free Press, 1988). Originally published as *L'homme et le sacré* (Paris: Gallimard, 1939).

16. See Peter Bürger, *Ursprung des postmodernen Denkens* (Weilerswist: Velbrück Wissenschaft, 2000).

17. Rudolf Otto, *The Idea of the Holy: An Inquiry into the Non-rational Factor in the Idea of the Divine and Its Relation to the Rational*, trans. John W. Harvey (Harmondsworth: Penguin, 1959). Originally published as *Das Heilige. Über das Irrationale in der Idee des Göttlichen und sein Verhältnis zum Rationalen* (Munich: Beck, 1917).

18. Peter Brunner, "Der Begriff der Religion bei William James und bei Rudolf Otto," *Theologische Blätter* 7 (1928): 97–104.

19. Otto, *Idea of the Holy*, 24.

20. Ibid., 25.

21. His most accessible book is: Mircea Eliade, *The Sacred and the Profane: The Nature of Religion* (New York and Evanston, IL: Harper and Row, 1957).

22. Max Scheler, *On the Eternal in Man*, trans. Bernard Noble (London: SCM Press, 1960); Max Scheler, "Probleme der Religion. Zur religiösen Erneuerung" (1920), in *Vom Ewigen im Menschen*, vol. 5 of his *Gesammelte Schriften* (Bern: Francke, 1954), 105–356; on Otto, see 285ff., on James 291f.

23. John Dewey, *A Common Faith* (New Haven, CT: Yale University Press, 1934).

24. Talcott Parsons, *Action Theory and the Human Condition* (New York: Free Press, 1978), 167ff. These studies remain almost unknown. For a recent

treatment, see Hans Joas, "The Gift of Life: The Sociology of Religion in Talcott Parsons' Late Work," *Journal of Classical Sociology* 1 (2001): 127–141.

25. Clifford Geertz, "Religion as a Cultural System," in *The Interpretation of Cultures* (London: Hutchinson and Co., 1975), 87–125; the way in which developments in symbolic theory have changed how scholars study conversion in comparison with James is clearly apparent in Monika Wohlrab-Sahr, *Konversion zum Islam in Deutschland und USA* (Frankfurt am Main: Campus, 1999).

26. Ibid., 119ff.

27. Ibid., 120.

28. A good overview can be found in Robert Wuthnow, "Sociology of Religion," in Neil Smelser, ed., *Handbook of Sociology* (London: Sage, 1989), 473–509.

29. See, for instance, Peter L. Berger, *A Far Glory: The Quest for Faith in an Age of Credulity* (New York: Free Press, 1992). For an attempt to get to grips with his ideas, see the chapter "Religion in the Age of Contingency" in this volume.

30. Of the extensive literature on this topic, the following work is particularly important: R. Stephen Warner, "Work in Progress Toward a New Paradigm for the Sociological Study of Religion in the United States," *American Journal of Sociology* 98 (1993): 1044–1093; Philip Gorski, "Historicizing the Secularization Debate," *American Sociological Review* 65 (2000): 138–167.

31. See, for example, Thomas Luckmann, *The Invisible Religion: The Problem of Religion in Modern Society* (New York: MacMillan, 1967).

32. The following study, which is international and comparative in nature, deals with this subject in masterful fashion: José Casanova, *Public Religions in the Modern World* (Chicago: University of Chicago Press, 1994). Another volume full of stimulating ideas is Wolfgang Huber, *Kirche in der Zeitenwende* (Gütersloh: Bertelsmann Stiftung, 1998). Just how complex these matters can be is apparent in the following outstanding study: Berit Bretthauer, *Televangelismus in den USA. Religion zwischen Individualisierung und Vergemeinschaftung* (Frankfurt and New York: Campus, 1999).

33. Robert Bellah, *Beyond Belief*; Bellah, *Tokugawa Religion* (Glencoe, IL: Free Press, 1957); Bellah, *The Broken Covenant* (New York: Seabury, 1975). Particularly important from a theoretical point of view is his essay "Religious Evolution," in *Beyond Belief*, 20–50.

5

Sophisticated Fundamentalism from the Left? On John Milbank

In the middle of the 1960s, Talcott Parsons—undoubtedly the world's most important sociologist in the first decades after World War II, and at that time at the peak of his influence and reputation—took part in a debate about the relationship between theology and sociology. His contribution, later published in a volume called *America and the Future of Theology*,[1] was a fervent plea for the significance of sociology in front of a theological audience. But not everybody in this audience seems to have accepted his arguments. The theological commentator at the debate, Oliver Read Whitley, made it abundantly clear in his response that the wedding of the two disciplines that Parsons had suggested should not take place immediately. Its announcement should at least be postponed until certain matters of vital importance for the marriage would have been cleared up. He emphasized that if we assume that one of the crucial conditions of a happy marriage lies in the equal chances of the partners to talk to each other, then the marriage Parsons had proposed would probably not be successful. The dialogue between the partners could, under Parsons's conditions, only be "a conversation in which the social sciences speak and theology listens, afterwards hastening to adapt its views to what the social sciences have stated."[2] Theology thus would be a mostly "passive" or "dependent" partner and not a "fully participating equal colleague."

John Milbank's writings, particularly his brilliant book *Theology and Social Theory,* do not offer us the perspective of a happy marriage either. Frustrated and even outraged by a world in which, if not sociology, then certainly the sciences or at least "secular reason" have the say, he does not put much effort into an attempt to carefully delineate the possibilities and the limits of communication and cooperation between theology and the social sciences. Instead, he turns the tables and declares theology to be the master discourse of the future. He repudiates the claims of sociology to present an adequate view of reality and thus to define a place even for the sacred, and tries to get beyond what he calls the "false humility" of theologians today. The social sciences, according to Milbank, are bound to a project of secular reason—without being able to self-reflectively understand what the historical conditions for the constitution of this seemingly self-evident notion and sphere of the "secular" were. "Once, there was no 'secular'"[3] is the forceful opening sentence of his book. Not only sociology but also liberal political philosophy, political economy, Hegelian and Marxist philosophy of history, and postmodern philosophy and cultural studies—they all become the object of Milbank's mostly devastating critiques; they all seem to suffer from the same birth defect and to be doomed to perish in view of the revitalized theology or the revitalized Catholic thinking that Milbank so powerfully propagates and that he intends to develop into the "ultimate" social science (6).

This is certainly a highly provocative thesis, and a discussion of it is a challenge—not only because of the enormous breadth of Milbank's scholarship and the sweeping claims he constantly makes, but also because his argument touches the self-understanding of theologians and of all those sociologists who are not willing to completely compartmentalize their religious and their scientific identities. Judging from the number of sociological reviews, however, there don't seem to be many who have taken Milbank's challenge seriously, and Milbank's very polemical tone in his all-out attack on sociology as such has certainly not motivated sociologists to deal with his work. In theology, on the other hand, the book has been called "perhaps the most brilliant, ambitious—and yet questionable—work to have emerged in English theology since the Second World War"[4]—by the same reviewer, incidentally, who warns the readers of Milbank's "sophisticated fundamentalism."⁵ Another reviewer speaks of an "imposing book of Blumenbergian proportions,"⁶ and I have no doubt that one can indeed place the book in one league with works by Hans Blumenberg, Charles Taylor, and Alasdair MacIntyre—authors Milbank often mentions—but also with books by Karl Löwith and Max Scheler, authors who are conspicuously absent from Milbank's work. I mention Löwith because one could claim that Milbank's insistence on the fact that many concepts and intellectual approaches of modernity can be traced back to a process of secularization is much closer to Löwith's attack on than to Blumenberg's defense of the "legitimacy of the modern age"; and I mention Scheler because he had a missionary zeal similar to Milbank's to finally formulate in appropriate philosophical ways what the Christian idea of love is all about. But to take up Milbank's challenge does not mean to surrender to his conclusions. I will have to be selective in my critique because of the almost encyclopedic range of Milbank's text, but I will try to demonstrate in six steps why I think his argument is deeply and seriously flawed. Milbank, I will show, distorts the sociological views of religion and ignores large parts of the sociological heritage that would be relevant for his questions. He thus misses the opportunity to build on an important type of knowledge and opens the door for a sociologically uninformed radical rhetoric, making it more difficult to enter into a fruitful dialogue between theologians and social scientists—whether they are believers or not. Such a dialogue, however, which does not have to lead to a marriage of the disciplines, could be an important prototype for reasonable communication about differing ultimate value commitments in the modern world.

Let me start with a point about which Milbank and I probably are in agreement. It is undoubtedly true that the founding fathers of sociology mostly assumed that a process of secularization is a corollary of the process of modernization, and they shared this often unstated assumption with many representatives of other academic disciplines and other intellectuals of their time. "In one form or another, with the possible exception of Alexis de Tocqueville, Vilfredo Pareto, and William James, the thesis of secularization was shared by all founding fathers from Karl Marx to John Stuart Mill, from Auguste Comte to Herbert Spencer, from E. B. Tylor to James Frazer, from Ferdinand Tönnies to Georg Simmel, from Émile Durkheim to Max Weber, from Wilhelm Wundt to Sigmund Freud, from Lester Ward to William G. Sumner, from Robert Park to George H.

Mead. Indeed, the consensus was such that not only did the theory remain uncontested, but apparently it was not even necessary to test it, since everybody took it for granted."[7] In most cases, this premise was the basis for the ideas these authors had about the possible functions of religion, and it definitely makes sense to examine how basic theoretical assumptions of sociology and its whole conceptual apparatus depend on this untenable assumption. And untenable this assumption is. For a long time, cases of enduring religious vitality have been interpreted as exceptional, as deviating from the normal course of modernization—so that Poland and Ireland might have escaped the forces propelling secularization because of the fusion of religion with the struggles for national and cultural independence there. The most spectacular case has, of course, been the United States—but here again the religious life has been seen as part of U.S. exceptionalism in general. Yet there is a growing consensus in the sociology of religion that the U.S. case has to be taken more seriously. If the currently prevailing explanation of continuing U.S. religious vitality is correct—the hypothesis, namely, that it is mostly religious pluralism and the strict separation of church and state that keep politically disgruntled believers in the religious "sector" of a society[8]—then secularization should no longer be considered one of the components of modernization but only a contingent process, owing to some extent to European traditions of territorial church monopoly and the fusion of political and ecclesiastical interests. The more recent "modernization" of parts of the world whose cultures are not based on the Judeo-Christian tradition has given additional strength to the assumption that perhaps continental Europe, not the United States, is the exception. In view of the current resurgence of religion in large parts of the world, Peter Berger now even speaks of the "desecularization of the world."[9]

Secularization in the sense of necessary religious decline thus clearly is no longer the ruling paradigm in the sociology of religion. But the concept of secularization is not unambiguous. There are also authors who do not use it as a label for religious decline or for a complete privatization of religion—which would also be empirically untenable[10]—but for a process of functional differentiation between societal subspheres, which makes it necessary for religion to adapt, to redefine its place in a social order in which no societal subsphere can reign supreme. And it is here, in the second step, that the disagreement between Milbank and me becomes visible; this also made it important for me to begin with the distinction of the different meanings the notion of "secularization" has.

It is absolutely crucial for Milbank's argument to show that secularization in the sense of functional differentiation, that is, as the rise of new spheres of desacralized politics and depoliticized religion, is itself a process of institutionalization and not the mere liberation of a formerly latent force of the secular that came into its own as soon as "the pressure of the sacred was relaxed." I fully agree with him when he writes: "The secular as a domain had to be instituted or *imagined,* both in theory and in practice. This institution is not correctly grasped in merely negative terms as a desacralization" (9). And I share his resistance to the term *secularization* for this process if it is meant as "a metaphor of the removal of the superfluous and additional to leave a residue of the human, the natural and the self-sufficient" (ibid.). But I sharply disagree with him not only when he adds immediately that "received sociology altogether misses the positive institution of the secular" (an evaluation to which I will return shortly), but, above all, when he seems to assume that an analysis of the institutionalization of the "secular" somehow shatters its claims to validity. Though Milbank calls his own endeavor *archeological,* I would say that the appropriate term for it would be *genealogical*—in the sense in which Nietzsche and Foucault used this notion to characterize their own critical efforts. But in my eyes, it is completely mistaken to assume that a demonstration of the contingent—that is, nonnatural and nonnecessary—character of a phenomenon can in any way diminish the claims it incorporates. Against Milbank's "genealogical" analysis, I would defend Charles Taylor's "anti-genealogy of morals,"[11] that is, the idea that our deepest value commitments always have to be articulated in narrative form and that we live amid such narratives so that the narrative of the rise of a secular sphere can as well be read as the narrative leading to our commitment to defend such a sphere, even as believers, against the imposition of religious convictions on nonbelievers and other societal spheres. Milbank goes so far as to call (15) "the space in which there *can be* a 'secular'" "fictional," "just as fictional as all other human topographies." But I doubt that one can use the word *fictional* here without becoming self-contradictory, because the word *fiction* presupposes a contrast with *nature* or *reality,* which loses its sense when we consider all institutions the result of creative processes of institutionalization.[12] And I find it even worse when Milbank calls the famous formula of Hugo Grotius *etsi Deus non daretur*—which played such an important role in the modern transformation of natural law—a "ruse" (10), without being able to see it as an offer for the carving out of a sphere for reasonable argument between different sorts of believers.

I would like to be very clear at this point. Milbank is right when he opposes "the facile theme of 'secularization'" (28) if this means a mere transfer of concepts like "voluntarist sovereignty" "from God and the sacred to the human and secular," and when he suggests instead "that *only* the theological model permits one to construct the *mythos* of the sovereign power, or sovereign person, so that it is not a case of 'essentially' secular and pragmatic realities being temporarily described in antique theological guise." He even sees that it was "in the midst of the crisis posed by religious conflict [that] Bodin and Hobbes contrived solutions at once sacred and pragmatic, founded upon a new metaphysics of political power." And one can further agree with him that "it is when theology finally *drops out of* modern theories of sovereignty that the real moment of mystification occurs, because here the 'mythical' character of sovereignty is forgotten." But doesn't that mean that Hobbes's own mythological construction could still be defended if we take the experiences of religious conflict seriously from which it arose? That exactly is my point. Though I find it justified and fruitful to use a strong notion of "secularization" as John Milbank does here—thus, incidentally, being closer to Carl Schmitt than to Hans Blumenberg—I cannot accept the way in which for him this includes the assumption that mankind went astray when it followed that path. Empirically, it is not correct to assume that the depoliticization of religion after the religious wars and civil wars of the early modern age could only lead to complete privatization of religion and a public sphere devoid of all religious symbols and religiously grounded manifestations. On the contrary, the precise character of the delimitation between the political and the religious, or, I should say, between obligatory public regulation and the voluntary manifestation of belief, will always remain contested and never become definitively fixed. And normatively religious freedom can be seen as the corollary of secularization in this sense of functional differentiation. Such religious freedom has been considered a value in itself by some types of Protestantism, like Quakerism, since the eighteenth century and even by the Catholic Church since the Second Vatican Council. A similar positive attitude can apply to other results of functional differentiation like the separation of markets from many forms of political intervention. Here also, Milbank seems to assume that his demonstration of the contingent character of capitalism (36) will cast doubt on the justification of partially autonomous market mechanisms. But in most countries, the British-U.S. idea of markets as a sort of released nature played no role anyway—without this hampering the idea that it could be good for economic efficiency to allow markets to play their role. By wrongly assuming that his genealogical analyses of political theology, political economy, and sociology lead to a sort of Christian ideology critique that ushers in a new era free from the assumptions of modernity, Milbank comes to the rather appalling statement with which his first chapter ends: "It follows that if Christianity seeks to find a place for secular reason, it may be perversely compromising with what, on its own terms, is either deviancy or falsehood" (23).

My alternative approach would consider the processes of differentiation as the result of institutionalization processes that cannot be understood exclusively as the emanation of semantic changes or as the consequences of social-structural forces. We have to trace them back instead to individual and collective *experiences* and to the *articulation* and *interpretation* of these experiences. And here, I have to point to another major difference between Milbank and myself, which I would like to present at first in theological terms before I demonstrate the far-reaching consequences it has for our different appreciation of the sociological heritage. In his book, Milbank makes some very strong statements against the notion of "religious experience," for example with respect to so-called biblical sociology, that is, the use of sociological means to illuminate the scriptures and biblical history, when he flatly denies a "pre-textual genesis" and writes: "social genesis itself is an 'enacted' process of reading and writing" (114). These statements could be and have been understood (or misunderstood) as the expression of an extreme version of text-based theology, as an attempt to silence all personalized encounters with the sacred texts, and as a reduction of theology's function so as "to 'persuade' us to absolute submission to the universal dominium of a particular ecclesiastical rule."[13] In his response to critics, Milbank had not only some beautiful things to say about the experience of faith as trust in the unknown, "as an active, joyful, erotic risk ... in the mode of hopeful delight in the unknown,"[14] but also made clear that his conception of theology does not "exclude the experiential and ineffable although it does, indeed, deny that experience is first of all inarticulate and personal."[15] I find it a deep insight when he emphasizes how "experience" and "articulation" are intertwined; that means that we identify an experience as an experience paradoxically because we face the difficulty of articulation. In Milbank's words: "Experience arrives at the event of an articulation."[16] The difference between him and me thus is not simply the difference between an "experiential-expressive" and a "cultural-linguistic" view of religious experience, because both of us accept the complex interplay among experience, articulation, and available cultural patterns. But the difference becomes visible when—in a move reminiscent of his "genealogy of the secular"—Milbank interprets the fact that the concept of "religious experience" is indeed a product of the nineteenth century as an indication that this notion "confines religious experience to the private sublime margins and so 'polices' it."[17] Again, Milbank seems to be unable to see in the conceptual change that took place between Schleiermacher and William James a probably irreversible expression of the individualization of religion. The problem I have is twofold. First, to say that there is no "prior" experience of God and Jesus in the Christian world, independent of religious narrative and doctrine, is correct, but it does not imply that people could not defend their articulations of such an experience against others and, above all, against official doctrines. And second, to say that "religious experience" is a modern notion does not disqualify it from being an appropriate point of departure for the understanding of modern religious experience and, for that matter, even for the uncovering of important dimensions of premodern religion. To insist on the experiential dimension of religion does not mean that one naively ascribes a foundational role to a completely inarticulate experience,[18] nor does it imply that such experience is necessarily purely individual, detached from others, from collectivities, and religious institutions.

And this brings me to our different appreciation of the sociological heritage. I deeply believe that it is the notion of experience that gives access to the most fruitful tradition in the sociological study of religion. It was, of course, William James's Gifford lectures, published in 1902 as *The Varieties of Religious Experience,* that constituted the revolutionary breakthrough in this direction—though its exclusive emphasis on individual experience as an experience in one's solitude seldom went unnoticed. A whole generation of intellectuals—including Martin Heidegger and Ludwig Wittgenstein, Georg Simmel and Max Scheler—felt deeply moved by this book. In German theology, it was Ernst Troeltsch who reviewed the book immediately and later came back to it repeatedly.[19] It was probably Troeltsch also who drew Max Weber's attention to James's work. The influence of James was even constitutive for Émile Durkheim's study of Australian totemism in *The Elementary Forms of Religious Life* (in 1912),[20] which one should interpret not merely as an attempt to demonstrate the socially integrative function of religion but much more as a theory of religion based on the analysis of collective experience. Durkheim's work thus inspired not only later functionalist analyses of religion in the work of Edward Shils and Talcott Parsons but also the maverick endeavor of the French *Collège de Sociologie* in the 1930s around Georges Bataille and Roger Caillois. I will not go on developing my own narrative here of the relationship between social theory and religion in the twentieth century. I partly did that in my book *The Genesis of Values*,[21] which speaks about "values" in order to include the great secular quasi religions of the twentieth century like Marxism, Fascism, nationalism, and, yes, to some extent liberalism, if it is considered a doctrine of salvation. And I have in the meantime elaborated this theory further in order to explain the genesis of a crucial value complex of our time: the belief in human rights and human dignity. A sociological study of such a question is different from a mere rational, argumentative justification and a mere narration disconnected from questions of justification; it is the "anti-genealogy of morality" I claimed before, and it is such in a continuity with the sociological tradition that has always led to such attempts at "anti-genealogy."

But John Milbank has a different view. For him, the main alternative in secular social theory seems to lie between positivism and Marxism (260). This sounds like the battle cries of the late 1960s. For him, all sociology is deeply permeated by the spirit of positivism; for him, sociology in its classic forms thus is itself a form of heretic theology, even a church in disguise. But although what he says is certainly true for the amateurish predecessors like Auguste Comte and Herbert Spencer and for the self-understanding of many empirical social researchers, it is a complete exaggeration and serious distortion if one generalizes this view so that it includes the classics of the field and professional social theorists. I do not want to bother nonsociologists with too many detailed refutations of Milbank's claims and to appear as a nit-picking enthusiast upset by an attack on his beloved area of specialization. So just consider the following brief list of examples.

The historiography of sociology since Parsons[22] distinguishes between the forerunners of the discipline and the classics like Max

Weber, Georg Simmel, Émile Durkheim, and George Herbert Mead. Although the forerunners were positivists, the classics were sharply critical of them. Although both Durkheim and Simmel clearly had a positivist background, they grew away from it. Max Weber never was a positivist; though Milbank discusses the influence of Neo-Kantianism on Weber, he ignores the wider field of influences from Nietzsche on the one hand and Dilthey on the other. Mead never was a positivist either, but is one of the crucial figures of pragmatism. Parsons was never a positivist. He was deeply influenced by Whitehead's philosophy,[23] and his understanding of the logic of theory construction has been claimed as an early case of post-positivist epistemology.[24] So to criticize positivism in order to criticize sociology clearly will not do.

This constitutive simplification in his approach to sociology distorts Milbank's interpretations of all the main authors. In his sub-chapter on Max Weber, he makes some very perceptive points about the influence of a Protestant meta-narrative on Weber's reconstruction of religious history, for example his views on the Reformation, on Jewish history, and his notion of "disenchantment." The inappropriateness of Weber's views on Catholicism had earlier been pointed out,[25] and in recent years thorough studies of Weber's theological sources[26] have produced a wealth of insights confirming some of Milbank's hunches. But although it is correct to criticize the implicit secularism of the "disenchantment" thesis, one should not misunderstand—as Milbank does—the main trait of Weber's work, namely, to offer a story in which modern secular rationalism is traced back to its religious roots. This is rather similar to Milbank's own efforts. It is true that Weber's statements are couched in terms of tragedy: Religious forces, according to him, brought about a regime that does not allow these religious forces to remain forceful. But Weber's historical predictions have not proven to be correct. To say it in a shorthand formula[27]: We can liberate Georg Jellinek's thesis of the Protestant origins of our belief in human rights from the Weberian framework; we can see it not as a charismatization of reason—as Weber did—but as a charismatization of the person. Ernst Troeltsch, in particular, had a more complex view than Max Weber about the possible role of Christianity and religion in modernity. He knew that it is possible to develop productive reinterpretations of the Judeo-Christian tradition, find new experiential bases for individualistic beliefs and new organizational structures, synthesizing traits from churches, sects, and individual spirituality of mysticism. This allowed Troeltsch to reinterpret Christianity as a stronghold of the sacralization of the individual, every individual human being, against the depersonalizing forces of modernity. This would neither be the easy compromise between religion and modernity nor its antithetical opposition. I do not understand how Milbank comes to the assertion that both Troeltsch and Weber made the claim that a social factor is "universally the prime determinant of the religious ethos itself" (98). Weber had a dualistic, not a monocausal attitude here, and Troeltsch was very explicit in his direct opposition to what Milbank assumes to be his position.[28]

Regarding Durkheim, Milbank first of all brings up again the old myth of the origins of sociology in French counter-Enlightenment thinking and counterrevolutionary politics—a myth finally put to rest by Johan Heilbron's studies on French social thought prior to the Revolution.[29] He then exaggerates the positivist character of Durkheim's work and the degree to which his work contributes to a sacralization of the (French) nation-state. Again, I am ready to admit that a closer study of Durkheim's work in the context of Jewish and Catholic religious debates has to be undertaken.[30] But one should not fail to notice that for Durkheim, as an ardent defender of "human rights," the sacralization of the individual person gets priority over any sacralization of the state, so that his nationalism is always couched in universalist terms. And I have already mentioned that, for me, Durkheim's true achievement in the study of religion, namely, the study of collective experience, is completely missing in Milbank's account.

Even more spectacular than the foregoing omissions are the two that I mention next. In the whole chapter on Parsons, Milbank never even mentions the rich series of contributions Parsons delivered in the last decade of his life to the sociological study of Christianity and the idea of the "gift of life" as, in Parsons's words, the mythical core of the Judeo-Christian tradition.[31] And though Milbank calls himself a pragmatist, his reference is Maurice Blondel and none of the authors everybody else considers the leading thinkers of pragmatism. Aside from a very superficial passage on G. H. Mead, Milbank has nothing to say about the most important philosophical undercurrent of pre-Parsonian U.S. sociology. The name of William James is not mentioned once, and the relationship between Blondel's "supernatural pragmatism" and U.S. pragmatism remains completely unclear.[32]

This might be sufficient to substantiate my harsh criticism of Milbank's picture of sociology. I will not continue discussing the question of whether Milbank's picture of Hegelianism, Marxism, and postmodernism is similarly distorted. More important for my argument is that Milbank, by offering such a distorted picture, cuts himself off, not merely from the rich tradition of sociological theory but also from the empirical research based on it. The hubris of his claims for theology as the "ultimate social science" becomes evident when one observes how empirically uncontrolled his remarks on social reality are. The political message of Milbank's theological orthodoxy is Christian socialism! Milbank knows that some of his readers will be surprised, and he confesses to being aware of the danger that his theological positions might be perceived to put him on the side of the "Vatican reactionaries." Milbank has been criticized[33] for the general elusiveness of his institutional proposals, whether they refer to the internal structures of the Church, to Church-State relationships, or to the political structures of a society organized along the principles of his Christian socialism. His critics should not allow him to get away with the old excuse that the movement or the community itself will develop the alternatives, because against this the old conservative principle seems to hold that those who make a proposal for change have to bear the burden of proof.

The other side of this elusiveness regarding his institutional proposals is the radical tone of Milbank's rhetoric concerning the present order. He uses the antiglobalization slogan of the present "neo-liberal" order[34] and calls "the new global sway of neo-capitalism ... which is the source of the hunger of the poor, the poisoning of nature, obliteration of sexual difference and equality, the lapse of beauty, the loss of historical memory and so on and so forth."[35] He does not even try to use social-scientific knowledge about the rather ambivalent consequences of globalization and about the social causes of poverty or environmental problems. His attacks on capitalism *and* bureaucracy at once sound like old style critical theory, and Milbank might be one of the last authors to speak of "late capitalism"[36] after the collapse of communism. He is proud to be "one of the few people continuing to uphold the bare possibility of a 'radicalism.'"[37] Notions like "the oppressed" and "violence" appear frequently, but their usage is as vague as it is in much current academic radicalism.

He even calls the present order a "more subtle totalitarianism" and envisages a post-liberal age. I do know that everybody who criticizes such radical rhetoric is easily perceived as complacent, satisfied with the present world order, and ignorant of its severe deficiencies.

But if you allow me to refer to my German background here, I would rather claim a post-totalitarian liberalism—a liberalism that has gone through the experience of the two main versions of totalitarianism—than a facile "post-liberal" attitude. And whoever calls the Western democracies a more subtle form of totalitarianism does not know what totalitarianism is.

Now, Milbank has undoubtedly the right to his political convictions. My point here is not simply that they seem to be different from my own convictions, but that he does not even enter into the attempt to demonstrate how his "ultimate social science" leads to the conclusions he draws. Compared with the social sciences and the professional ethos there to offer empirical support for one's theoretical claims or to examine them empirically, his views are a clear overextension of a theological discourse. Theology and the social sciences will not come into a happy marriage on Milbank's conditions. This is not surprising, because Milbank has always seen the relationship in agonistic terms and even proclaimed the end of dialogue between the partners. For him, the goal of conversion should not be taken out of the conversation.

In my perspective, the crass opposition between attempts to convert on the one hand and mere rational discourse on the other also stems from the relative neglect of the experiential dimension in Milbank's thought. If we remain on the level of doctrine, we can only imagine mutual exclusion or pseudo-rational attempts to prove the superiority of one's own belief. But if we recognize the importance of religious experience, we tend to assume that there is indeed something we can learn from our partner in a conversation. Where else should the curiosity to learn from others come from? It leads to modesty concerning the range of one's own experiences. And it leads to an openness toward what Charles Taylor calls in his lecture "A Catholic Modernity?" the "humbling realization that modern culture, in breaking with the structures and beliefs of Christendom, also carried certain facets of Christian life further than they were ever taken or could have been taken within Christendom."[38]

Now, I don't want to push Milbank completely in the direction of Catholic triumphalism. I find it important when he replies to a Jewish critic that religious toleration can indeed not only be founded on secular rationalism but also on Christianity, and he mentions "some Christian humanists, some 17th-century puritans, some 18th-century Anglicans of a perfectly orthodox cast [who] argued that Christian belief of its nature requires absolutely free assent, and that the light of the gospel was only able to manifest itself in the relatively free and open period of late antiquity."[39] And he even claims: "Pluralism is far better upheld by Christians than by Enlightenment." I doubt that the historical record supports this statement empirically, but I see the normative impulse behind this statement, and I sympathize with it. Nevertheless, and ignoring possible inconsistencies between these declarations and the thrust of Milbank's big book, it misses the crucial controversial point when Milbank argues here for a possible theological justification of religious freedom. Because as valid as this justification might be for believers, we still need to accept that others find other justifications convincing, given their religious or secular premises. But this would mean a religious acceptance also of secular justifications of the secular sphere—something Milbank abhors. It would be along the lines of the famous preamble of the Polish constitution—that believers come to it one way and nonbelievers the other way, but both agree in their commitment to its principal values and procedures. That seems to me to be the true prospect for fruitful communication. In that sense, the dialogue between theology and social theory is similar to the dialogues going on between the proponents of different value commitments within social theory. There can be and has to be a sphere for the peaceful and mutually enriching communication between values, the related narratives, and practices. John Milbank's intense effort to make theology and Catholic thinking play an important role in such a dialogue again is enormously welcome. But his tendencies to overextend his claims and the antiliberal and anti-empirical undertones of his work are in danger of increasing the intellectual isolation from which Milbank set out to release theology.

NOTES

1. Talcott Parsons, "Social Science and Theology," in William A. Beardslee, ed., *America and the Future of Theology* (Philadelphia: Westminster Press, 1967), 136–157.

2. Oliver Read Whitley, "Questions to Talcott Parsons," ibid., 165–173, here 170.

3. John Milbank, *Theology and Social Theory: Beyond Secular Reason* (Oxford: Blackwell, 1990), 9; subsequent page references in the text refer to this book.

4. Richard H. Roberts, "Transcendental Sociology? A Critique of John Milbank," *Scottish Journal of Theology* 46 (1993): 527–535, here 527.

5. Ibid., 534.

6. Bruce Krajewski, introduction to the Symposium on "Theology and Social Theory," *Arachne* 2 (1995): 105–108, here 108.

7. José Casanova, *Public Religions in the Modern World* (Chicago: University of Chicago Press, 1994), 17.

8. R. Stephen Warner, "Work in Progress Toward a New Paradigm for the Sociological Study of Religion in the United States," *American Journal of Sociology* 98 (1993): 1044–1093.

9. Peter L. Berger, ed., *The Desecularization of the World: Resurgent Religion and World Politics* (Washington, DC: Eerdmans, 1999); see the introduction by Berger (1–18) and Grace Davie, "Europe: The Exception That Proves the Rule?" (65–84).

10. This is the main point of Casanova's book (see fn. 7), on whose distinction of different meanings of "secularization" I rely.

11. I take this expression from a review of Charles Taylor's *Sources of the Self* by Martin Seel, "Die Wiederkehr der Ethik des guten Lebens," *Merkur* 45 (1991): 42–49, here 49.

12. See Hans Joas, "Institutionalization as a Creative Process: The Sociological Importance of Cornelius Castoriadis' Political Philosophy," *American Journal of Sociology* 94 (1988/89): 1184–1199, reprinted in Hans Joas, *Pragmatism and Social Theory* (Chicago: University of Chicago Press, 1993), 154–171.

13. E.g., Eve Tavor Bannet, "Beyond Secular Theory," *Arachne* 2 (1995): 109–115.

14. John Milbank, "On Theological Transgression," *Arachne* 2 (1995): 145–176, here 154.

15. Ibid., 164.

16. Ibid.

17. Ibid.

18. This point has been forcefully argued by Richard Shusterman against Richard Rorty's interpretation of Dewey in Richard Shusterman, "Dewey on Experience: Foundation or Reconstruction?" *The Philosophical Forum* 26 (1994): 127–148.

19. Ernst Troeltsch, review of James in *Deutsche Literaturzeitung* 25 (1904): 3021–3027; Ernst Troeltsch, "Empiricism and Platonism in the Philosophy of Religion—To the Memory of William James," in *Harvard Theological Review* 5 (1912): 401–422.

20. Émile Durkheim, *Les formes élémentaires de la vie religieuse* (Paris: Alcan, 1912).

21. Hans Joas, *The Genesis of Values* (Chicago: University of Chicago Press, 2000).

22. Talcott Parsons, *The Structure of Social Action* (New York: McGraw Hill, 1937).

23. Harald Wenzel, *Die Ordnung des Handelns. Talcott Parsons' Theorie des allgemeinen Handlungssystems* (Frankfurt am Main: Suhrkamp, 1991).

24. Jeffrey Alexander, *Theoretical Logic in Sociology*, vol. 1, *Positivism, Presuppositions, and Current Controversies* (Berkeley: University of California Press, 1982).

25. Werner Stark, "The Place of Catholicism in Max Weber's Sociology of Religion," *Sociological Analysis* 29 (1968): 202–210.

26. For example Friedrich Wilhelm Graf, "The German Theological Sources and Protestant Church Politics," in Hartmut Lehmann and Günther Roth, eds., *Weber's Protestant Ethic: Origin, Evidence, Context* (Cambridge: Cambridge University Press, 1987), 27–50.

27. For a longer version see my "Max Weber and the Origin of Human Rights: A Study of Cultural Innovation," in Charles Camic et al., eds., *Max Weber's "Economy and Society": A Critical Companion* (Stanford, CA: Stanford University Press, 2005), 366–382.

28. I call Weber's distinction between "ideas" and "interests" dualistic despite the fact that Weber was, of course, mostly interested in their combination. Ernst Troeltsch explicitly repudiated the claim he purportedly makes in the introduction to: Ernst Troeltsch, *Die Soziallehren der christlichen Kirchen und Gruppen*, 2 vols. (Tübingen: Mohr, 1912).

29. Johan Heilbron, *The Rise of Social Theory* (Cambridge: Polity Press, 1995).

30. As Milbank demands in "On Theological Transgression," 172. The Jewish context has now been thoroughly studied by Ivan Strenski, *Durkheim and the Jews of France* (Chicago: University of Chicago Press, 1997), and Pierre Birnbaum, *Géographie de l'espoir* (Paris: Gallimard, 2004), 85–123.

31. Most of these studies have been collected in Talcott Parsons, *Action Theory and the Human Condition* (New York: Free Press, 1978). See, on these studies, Hans Joas, "The Gift of Life: The Sociology of Religion in Parsons' Late Work," *Journal of Classical Sociology* 1 (2001), 127–141.

32. See on this question Frederick J. D. Scott, S. J., "William James and Maurice Blondel," *The New Scholasticism* 32 (1958): 32–44.

33. Alan Shandro, "On the Politics of Postmodern Theology," *Arachne* 2 (1995): 136–144.

34. John Milbank, "On Theological Transgression," 151.

35. Ibid., 173.

36. Ibid., 156.

37. Ibid., 157.

38. Charles Taylor in James L. Heft, ed., *A Catholic Modernity?* (New York: Oxford University Press, 1999), 16.

39. For the Jewish critique, see Daniel Boyarin, "A Broken Olive Branch," *Arachne* 2 (1995): 124–130; for Milbank's response: "On Theological Transgression," 170.

6

A Catholic Modernity?
Faith and Knowledge
in the Work
of Charles Taylor

Since the publication of his magisterial book *The Sources of the Self* in 1989 at the latest, Charles Taylor's work has become well known and highly respected in philosophy and the social sciences the world over. Monographs and collections of critical articles on his work have begun to appear in the past few years; his reconstruction of the crucial values and value innovations characteristic of the Western tradition seems set to have a lasting and profound influence on intellectual life. Some readers of *Sources*, particularly its last few chapters, might have wondered how exactly Taylor's indirect plea for theism, which he makes there, might be related to his personal religious conviction. But the book itself and Taylor's publications in general make it rather difficult to answer this emerging question. As George Marsden remarks, "Only the most acute readers might surmise that the author is Catholic, if they did not know that already"[1] (87). Taylor's hesitation with regard to this issue is completely understandable. Another leading Christian philosopher of our time, Paul Ricoeur, did not incorporate those of his Gifford Lectures that included discussion of theological matters in the volume *Oneself As Another* because of his horror of the thought of being perceived as more of a "crypto-theologian" than a philosopher. Within philosophical and scientific discourse, arguments must indeed be developed with the intention of convincing everyone, irrespective of his religious or other commitments. But elucidating the relationship between knowledge and faith in Taylor's work is at least of importance to understanding his work in context, if not to determining what constitutes a viable conception of Christian thinking today.

The book *A Catholic Modernity*, though very small, illuminates these issues in a rich and rewarding manner. It grew out of a talk given by Taylor in 1996 as part of a lecture series at the University of Dayton, Ohio. This was explicitly conceived as an opportunity to invite prominent Catholic intellectual figures to reflect in personal terms on the issues outlined above. Taylor's lecture is introduced here by James Heft, a Marianist priest and representative of the host institution. Four distinguished scholars present their reactions to Taylor's lecture, and finally Taylor comments on these responses and provides some concluding reflections.

The centerpiece of the book is Taylor's lecture entitled "A Catholic Modernity?" (13–37). It is written in the style that has become Taylor's trademark: modest and dialogical, but forceful in its metaphorical creativity. Taylor's key literary device in this lecture is his introduction of Matteo Ricci, the famous Jesuit missionary in China four centuries ago. Ricci had set out to preach the Christian faith to the Chinese, but he became deeply impressed by Chinese religion and culture and discovered the intricacies of an enterprise that has been called "preaching wisdom to the wise" (F. Clooney). Taylor attempts to look at our modern civilization in a similar way, as "another of those great cultural forms that have come and gone in human history"; he invites us to think about "what it means to be a Christian here, to find our authentic voice in the eventual Catholic chorus" (15). He is fully aware that it is both easier and more difficult to see our own post-Enlightenment civilization as Ricci saw China. It is easier because our culture is still pervaded by Christian elements despite all secularization; we need not start from scratch when we reflect upon Christianity in our culture. But it is also more difficult because modernity, at least in Europe, is so often defined as anti-Christian. But such a dichotomous view, which implies that post- or anti-Christian modernity features no more than remnants of a Christian past, is misleading. Against this notion, Taylor defends his core thesis: "that in modern, secularist culture there are mingled together both authentic developments of the gospel, of an incarnational mode of life, and also a closing off to God that negates the gospel. The notion is that modern culture, in breaking with the structures and beliefs of Christendom, also carried certain facets of Christian life further than they ever were taken or could have been taken within Christendom. In relation to the earlier forms of Christian culture, we have to face the humbling realization that the breakout was a necessary condition of the development" (16). Taylor's thesis closely resembles the reform of Catholic self-understanding during the buildup to and course of the Second Vatican Council. The goal of total fusion of the Christian faith with a particular society is not only considered unrealistic but not worth pursuing, even danger- ous. Taylor's Catholicism accepts functional differentiation and the importance of a public sphere as "the locus of competing ultimate visions" (18). He goes so far as to send "a vote of thanks to Voltaire and others for (not necessarily wittingly) showing us this and for allowing us to live the gospel in a purer way, free of that continual and often bloody forcing of conscience which was the sin and blight of all those 'Christian' centuries" (ibid.).

This central thesis also explains the title of the book. Taylor is situating himself in continuity neither with the so-called Catholic modernism of the nineteenth and early twentieth centuries nor with pleas for a "modern Catholicism," whatever that might be. Rather, he defends the role of Catholicism within modernity, that is, the pluralistic discourse of the contemporary world.

Well, one might reply, that is fine for Taylor and the Catholic Church, but what does it add to this discourse? Is his move anything more than a belated adaptation of Catholicism to the world of liberal- ism and democracy? In the second part of his lecture, Taylor tackles these more far-reaching questions, and here his claims are certainly more controversial. Although secular humanists might accept, for example, that human rights might be based on elements of the Judeo-Christian tradition, and although they might also welcome a Catholic plea for pluralism, they continue to assume that "hu- man life is better off without transcendental vision altogether. The development of modern freedom is then identified with the rise of an exclusive humanism—that is, one based exclusively on a notion of human flourishing, which recognizes no valid aim beyond this" (19). From a Christian viewpoint, this secular humanist attitude is unacceptable; for Taylor, accepting this view would mean undergoing a "spiritual lobotomy." And he goes on to demonstrate that there is "something that matters beyond life, on which life itself originally draws" (20). This can, of course, easily be misunderstood as a reversal of the modern "affirmation of ordinary life," which Taylor himself described so sensitively in *The Sources of the Self.* But Taylor distinguishes very clearly between the alleged tendency for the avoidance of suffering to play an increasingly smaller role in public policy and "opening the way for the insight that more than life matters" (24). He is not going to convince anybody by rational means here, but he can at least expose the self-serving attitude of "secular humanists" blind to the possibility that their denial of transcendence might have destructive consequences. He outlines a dialectic of secular humanism. On the psychological level, this relates to the pitfalls of social reform or philanthropic action untempered by unconditional love for the beneficiaries and realistic pessimism about the human potential for change, and, in fact, based on utopian historical visions or moralistic expectations. On the philosophical level, a parallel dialectic is at work in the relationship between secular humanism and Nietzscheanism. Influenced by René Girard, Taylor speculates on the fascination with death and violence as "at base a manifestation of our nature as *homo religiosus*" (28). Embracing transcendence without returning to the fusion of faith and secular order is Taylor's way out of the present crisis of reason.

There is little disagreement among Taylor and the other contributors to the volume; the responses are more complementary than critical. George Marsden, a leading Protestant American historian, encourages Christian scholars to follow Taylor's example and deploy their religious faith in a similarly productive and visible manner in their work; Jean Bethke Elshtain supports Taylor's pluralism with reflections on Augustine's Trinitarian theology, which sees God as a unity in diversity and underlines that humans were created in his image. Rosemary Luling Haughton emphasizes contemporary activism, new mythologies (such as that of Tolkien), and the need for an anti-ascetic revision of our views of the Christian conception of life as something to be enjoyed. I found the contribution by William Shea the most stimulating. Shea, author of a remarkable book on the history of U.S. philosophy of religion,[2] adds important historical substance to Taylor's claims by elaborating their relationship to Catholic modernism and church doctrine. He supports Taylor's conclusions about the dialectics of secular humanism with critical reflections on John Dewey. At the end of the book, Taylor himself discusses his earlier critique of Foucault's deeply "anti-dialogical" philosophy and his resistance to the exclusion from the field of philosophy proper of the problem of moral motivation; he brings out how these issues are connected with his attempt "to change the agenda" (123) of contemporary thinking in ways that make it at least possible to articulate Christian motives.

This small book does far more than help contextualize Taylor's thinking. It addresses questions crucial to contemporary moral and religious debates in a thought-provoking manner. My only major critical question is whether Taylor's view of contemporary atheism is not far too optimistic. He sees atheism mostly in terms of secular humanism on the one hand and neo-Nietzscheanism on the other, and this might be true of the more or less secularized societies of Western Europe. But what about secularized post-communist societies, from East Germany to Russia (with the significant exception of Poland)? The value orientations prevailing in these countries are hardly best described as "secular humanism." We could be dealing here with a new version of a-religiosity and anti-religiosity, which cannot be conceived as a continuation of earlier Christian motives. Although it is often easy to reach a consensus on values in the case of "secular humanism," concerning human rights for example, in these societies the situation is far more complex. Believers, who are in the minority, might either be embattled or condescended to. Here, a dialogue between Christianity and Enlightenment might appear profoundly eccentric. These are not objections to Taylor's convincing arguments but matters that Taylor's Central European sympathizers cannot resist mentioning.

The second book discussed here[3] consists of lectures Taylor gave at the Vienna Institute for Human Sciences (*Institut für die Wissenschaften vom Menschen*) in 2000; these grew out of his Gifford Lectures in Edinburgh in 1999. Surely the most renowned lecture series on the topic of religion, for more than one hundred years, leading thinkers have used this opportunity to share their ideas in the philosophy of religion. Taylor uses William James's famous 1902 Gifford Lectures as a foil to bring out his ideas. The title *Varieties of Religion Today* recalls James's book *The Varieties of Religious Experience*. Taylor begins by discussing the sense that James's lectures have largely retained their freshness even after a century, "that this long-dead author is in striking ways a contemporary" (vii). This is doubtless due in part to James's genius; but also to developments in Western culture, which have to some extent brought it closer to James's perspective.

The first of the four lectures grapples with the concept of "religious experience," which characterizes the real methodological revolution of James's psychology of religion. James's focus on individual religious experience and his abstraction of institutions, the edifice of theological teachings as well as collective experiences, is inherently one-sided and has frequently been criticized; with great expertise, Taylor places this approach within the framework of the history of religion. Here, he eschews the common stereotype that sees the emphasis on individual religious experience exclusively as a beneficial (or damaging) outcome of the Reformation. He knows that as early as the High Middle Ages it is possible to observe "a steadily increasing emphasis on a religion of personal commitment and devotion over forms centered on collective ritual" (9). What mendicants and piety-focused movements began, certainly reached a new high point with the Reformation. "But this movement toward the personal, committed, inward didn't exist only in the Protestant Churches. There was a parallel development in the Counter-Reformation" (10), expressed in attempts "to regulate the lives of the laity according to more and more stringent models of practice" (10). Although James himself certainly did not have a clear view of these historic facts and although his emphasis on the experience of the Divine was driven by a strong impulse to resist an exclusive stress on commandments and the demands made of human beings by God, Taylor sees James's thought quite explicitly as a continuation of long-term tendencies within Christianity. But this does not resolve the question of whether concentrating on religious experience when analyzing religious phenomena might also produce a distorted picture. From a Catholic perspective, Taylor asserts, it quickly emerges that mediation by the institution of the church of the link between the believer and the Divine can have no real place in James's way of thinking. The life of the church is for James of secondary religious importance, a derivation of the primary religious experience; it is not regarded as constitutive, as enabling such experiences. Taylor's critique of James here is correct; but Taylor goes further still and imputes to James a concept of experience that treats experience as if it requires no formulation, as if it is conceivable at all outside of cultural models. This seems unfair to me. It is true that in his book on religion James failed to sufficiently analyze the interaction among experience, articulation, and cultural interpretive models.[4] But his other writings make it clear that he was very well aware how dependent experience is on interpretation, and vice versa.[5]

The second lecture deals with James's analysis of the "twice born," that is, those who do not simply live in a state of untroubled accordance with the world and the faith of their childhood, but rather, aware of suffering and evil and thus on the basis of a sense of melancholy, experience a new breakthrough to faith. Here again, Taylor delves deeper into history, the subject of modern melancholy in this case, than James himself did. I was very impressed by his warning, directed against Max Weber and Marcel Gauchet (41), not to interpret the history of religion "as though from the beginning we could see it as an answer to the inherent meaninglessness of things" (ibid.). This might well be to rush to the conclusion that a modern problem of meaning is an anthropological universal. The remainder of the lecture is devoted to reconstructing James's line of argument regarding the will or right to faith in his famous essay of 1897.[6] Taylor distinguishes between a weaker and stronger reading of James's argument. On the first view, James merely wished to repudiate the common notion that reason compels us to embrace agnosticism. On the second view, James went further; he, who could bring out the inner logic of conscious faith and conscious nonbelief like no other, wanted to demonstrate irrefutably the necessity of deciding. "James is our great philosopher of the cusp. He tells us more than anyone else about what it's like to stand in that open space and feel the winds pulling you now here, now there. He describes a crucial site of modernity and articulates the decisive drama enacted there" (59).

The third lecture is dedicated to a diagnosis of "religion today" and thus to the issue of what James can contribute to the interpretation of the present. In a manner reminiscent of Peter Berger, Taylor equates a situation in which one "decides," which we have just been discussing, with that of a spiritual "choice." But this implies a religious landscape that "will be less and less hospitable to collective connections" (64) and whose public sphere is becoming ever more secular and neutral. Taylor uses these ideas as a launchpad for a highly original typology of relations between political and religious communities. To do so, he draws on another classical figure, Émile Durkheim.

Durkheim, of course, very much building on James,[7] developed his theory of the elementary forms of religious life, in which collective ecstasy (or as he called it, collective "effervescence") took pride of place. For Durkheim, the existence of the church as an institution was a defining feature of religion. In Taylor's typology, the coexistence of church and state, with "the social sacred ... defined and served by the church" (75), is the true "Durkheimian situation." Political society might, in medieval fashion, be imagined as itself pervaded with sacredness; or in the Baroque sense, whose exponents tried, against processes of disenchantment, to cling to the quasi-sacred inviolability of hierarchical orders, but were forced to compromise when, for example, "also elements of functional justification began to creep in, where monarchical rule was argued to be indispensable for order, for example" (70). I fail to understand quite why Taylor describes this Baroque approach, which, after all, he has characterized as partially modern, as "paleo-Durkheimian." In any event, he further distinguishes from this a "neo-Durkheimian" and a "post-Durkheimian" path. The classic example of the former is the United States. There, the pluralism of religious denominations is firmly established historically. The separation of state and religion is necessarily bound up with this; on the other hand, through this separation, "the political entity can be identified with the broader, overarching 'church,' and this can be a crucial element in its patriotism" (75). This path makes it easy to maintain religious faith and religious practice within the process of modernization. The (mostly Catholic) "Baroque" orders, meanwhile, necessarily produced antireligious, militantly secularist counteracting forces. Finally, Taylor describes as post-Durkheimian more recent forms of society, "in which the spiritual dimension of existence is quite unhooked from the political" (76).

It is at this point that Taylor is able to relate his conception of burgeoning "expressive individualism," which he has developed extensively in other works, to the diagnosis of religion. The question that arises is whether the expressive individualists still feel the slightest need "[to embed] our link to the sacred in any particular broader framework, whether 'church' or state" (95). This is indeed of central importance. But I cannot see that Taylor really answers the question he himself has posed or even provides a substantial overview of the opportunities and risks associated with expressive individualism in the religious sphere. Although his references to expressive individualists' affinities with certain values, such as those of tolerance, are quite correct, it nonetheless remains an open question what role collective experiences play or are able to play in forging commitment to values among expressive individualists. We might, for example, ask how, under these circumstances, the value of universal human dignity can be articulated and institutionalized.[8]

We might also ask whether key contemporary religious processes can be expressed within the Taylorian typology in the first place. The Catholic Church in the United States was, for example, never part of a "paleo-Durkheimian" model of social order; it was never located entirely within the neo-Durkheimian order, because it was for a long time eyed with suspicion with regard to its loyalty to U.S. values and because it did in fact wish to transcend these values. Finally, the "post-Durkheimian notion of choosing to join a particular denomination because it is the right one for you [is] rather uncommon among Catholics."[9] This example might show that Taylor's productive emphasis on trends toward expressive individualism depends on thinking through, in far greater depth than occurs here, its potential in religious and political terms and in light of its tensions with other value orientations.

Like a coda, Taylor's book concludes with a short final section, a summarizing response to the question "So was James right?" For all its brilliant sensitivity, James's diagnosis, according to Taylor, is inadequate in three respects. First, Taylor considers a thoroughly "post-Durkheimian" world almost unimaginable. Collective forms of mediation between the individual and the Divine persist and are constituted in new ways: Individualistic routes to faith might even lead to the consolidation of strong religious communities. Second, the "neo-Durkheimian" model is still very much alive in varied forms of religiously based politics. And third, even religious life, which begins in a "moment of blinding insight" (116), often leads to demanding spiritual discipline and thus leaves behind views of the religious centered on emotion and inspiration. But Taylor winds up by acknowledging once again the validity of James's central insight: that we should take individual religious experience as our starting point, at least for the religious analysis of the present day.

As an interpretation of James, as Taylor himself concedes, his little book is certainly "idiosyncratic and selective" (vi). As a diagnosis of religion in outline, it is highly stimulating, but nonetheless disappointing in that it merely hints at but fails to tackle in depth a large number of topics. The two slim volumes dealt with here certainly provide us with more "food for thought" than the heavy tomes produced by some contemporary writers; but they also leave us hungry for more fully developed work from Taylor's pen.

NOTES

1. James L. Heft, ed., *A Catholic Modernity? Charles Taylor's Marianist Award Lecture* (New York: Oxford University Press, 1999); subsequent page references in the text refer to this book.

2. William Shea, *The Naturalists and the Supernatural: Studies in Horizon and an American Philosophy of Religion* (Macon, GA: Mercer, 1984).

3. Charles Taylor, *Varieties of Religion Today: William James Revisited* (Cambridge, MA: Harvard University Press, 2002); subsequent page references in the text refer to this book.

4. See my own comments, in Hans Joas, *The Genesis of Values* (Chicago: University of Chicago Press, 1997), 58–86, and esp. 107–109.

5. See, for example, William James, *Some Problems of Philosophy* (New York: Longmans, Green & Co., 1911), 149. For an interpretation of James's philosophy from this perspective, see William Joseph Gavin, *William James and the Reinstatement of the Vague* (Philadelphia: Temple University Press, 1992). For an overall examination of these themes, see also the chapter entitled "On the Articulation of Experience" in this volume.

6. William James, *The Will to Believe* (New York: Longmans, Green & Co., 1897).

7. On Durkheim's development of James's work and the relationship between their two conceptions, see Hans Joas, *The Genesis of Values*, 87–109. Another attempt to deal with this topic has recently appeared, though it refers neither to Taylor's nor the present author's previous publications: Sue Stedman Jones, "From 'Varieties' to 'Elementary Forms': William James and Émile Durkheim on Religious Life," *Journal of Classical Sociology* 3 (2003): 99–122.

8. For a recent take on this issue, see Hans Joas, "Max Weber and the Origin of Human Rights: A Study of Cultural Innovation," in Charles Camic et al., eds., *Max Weber's "Economy and Society": A Critical Companion* (Stanford, CA: Stanford University Press, 2005), 366–382.

9. I base my comments here on Frank Adloff, *Im Dienste der Armen. Katholische Kirche und amerikanische Sozialpolitik im 20. Jahrhundert* (Frankfurt and New York: Campus, 2003), 345–351; the quotation appears on p. 349.

7

God in France:
Paul Ricoeur
As Theoretical Mediator

On November 30, 1969, Michel Foucault was elected to the Collège de France; his defeated rival was Paul Ricoeur. Given the prevailing mood at the time, this decision on who should be granted France's highest academic honor came as no great surprise. Not only had Foucault gained advance backing from such influential figures as Claude Lévi-Strauss, Georges Dumézil, and Fernand Braudel, his work was also unmistakably in keeping with the structuralist wave that had swept through intellectual life and the political radicalisms inspired by the student rebellions of 1968. But Foucault's triumph was more than a defeat for Ricoeur by a rival with a quite different intellectual orientation whom he nonetheless respected. For many, it symbolized the definitive triumph of structuralism over hermeneutics and phenomenology. At a personal level, this was only the latest in a long line of humiliations that forced Ricoeur to the margins of intellectual life in his own country.

This gradual marginalization was surprising, because Ricoeur had been generally regarded as the rising star in the firmament of French philosophy in the early 1960s; it delayed and restricted this great thinker's reception in France and without question in Germany and other countries, too. The situation in France has changed completely since around 1990, at the very latest with the publication of *Soi-même comme un autre,* which in many respects represents the culmination of Ricoeur's life's work.[1] The recognition Ricoeur has now received has been all the greater for its belatedness. For a younger generation, who chose not to pursue structuralism and poststructuralism and brought about the interpretative and pragmatic turn in French philosophy, humanities, and social sciences, Ricoeur has become the key point of reference. Further to his widely read two-volume history of structuralism, François Dosse provided a cogent account of these more recent developments in a book dedicated to none other than Ricoeur; he has now produced a comprehensive, almost eight-hundred-page biography of the revered theorist.[2] But there is as yet little sign that these shifts in the intellectual climate in France have been adequately registered beyond its borders.

Ricoeur was an orphan. His mother died soon after his birth; his father fell in the great Battle of the Marne in September 1915. His grandparents and an unmarried aunt raised him in Rennes, in the strict spirit of French Calvinism. The biographical points of departure of Ricoeur's thinking thus consist of the tragic remembering of the catastrophe in the early twentieth century and a process of coming to terms with the tension between the emphasis on guilt-feelings and the Good News of Christianity. In Paris in the 1930s, Ricoeur made contact with the group around Gabriel Marcel, for which the term *Christian existentialist* has taken hold, and that around the journal *Esprit,* in which a young anticapitalist and antitotalitarian Catholicism found political expression. Many of the motifs that define Ricoeur's life's work—from the emphasis on dialogic intersubjectivity to the power of the promise to establish identity—are found here in embryonic form. But the young Ricoeur found too much exuberance and too little rigor in the philosophical language of personalism.

Husserl's phenomenology, which he studied while teaching in a grammar school in Colmar toward the end of the 1930s, was far better suited to his need for stringency. Ricoeur spent the summer of 1939 in Munich to improve his German; he only just managed to leave Germany before the war broke out. But the events of the war caught up with him all the more mercilessly with the German attack on France. As a mobilized reserve officer, he was taken prisoner and transported to Farther Pomerania (*Hinterpommern*), where he spent the next five years of his life in a succession of camps. The conditions were astonishing. The prisoners were allowed not only to read but

also to organize a program of lectures and form religious communities. Ricoeur studied all the German philosophy he could get his
hands on and translated into French Husserl's *Ideen zu einer reinen
Phänomenologie* (*Ideas Pertaining to a Pure Phenomenology*)—in the
margins of the German edition for want of paper.

Ricoeur returned to liberated France as a philosopher who knew
exactly what he wanted to achieve. Far from Paris, he turned his analyses of Gabriel Marcel and Karl Jaspers into books and pursued his
idea of a phenomenology of the will; this developed out of his prewar
work on the phenomenology of attention to become a multivolume
but ultimately uncompleted work. Like Maurice Merleau-Ponty in
his *Phenomenology of Perception,* which has certainly become more
famous, and like Max Scheler, Ricoeur took up Husserl's approach,
but applied it to topics that affect subjectivity with respect to its bodily,
finite constitution and perception in terms of its relevance to action.
Through this work and the publication of the translation of Husserl
prepared during his wartime captivity, Ricoeur became one of the
most important mediators of phenomenology in France. In 1956, after
eight years as a professor in Strasbourg, Ricoeur was appointed to the
Sorbonne in Paris. In his academic teaching and numerous articles on
current affairs, he proved hugely talented at opening up to non-French
intellectual traditions and to all currents of thought that seemed to
challenge the further development of his philosophy of subjectivity.
He produced meticulous interpretations and commentaries dealing
with Marx and Nietzsche, Freud and Lévi-Strauss. The burgeoning
structuralist theory of language in particular caused him to revise his
views, and although its focus on the internal systematics of language,
texts, and myths failed to make Ricoeur a convert to structuralism,
they did inspire his embrace of hermeneutics. According to him,
reflection upon oneself can succeed only via others and via the various ways in which subjectivity is realized. But unlike Heidegger and
Gadamer, Ricoeur was unwilling to pay for this hermeneutic turn
by distancing himself from the methodology of the humanities and
social sciences. For him, hermeneutically inclined phenomenology
must be suffused with science. This hermeneutic turn also opened up
new opportunities for Ricoeur to pursue his theological interests. The
existential interpretation of the New Testament by Rudolf Bultmann
served as a point of reference as he developed his own hermeneutics.
During this period Ricoeur became the leading intellectual exponent
of Protestantism in France.

The humiliations began in the mid-1960s. Ricoeur's dispute with Lévi-Strauss in 1963 stirred up intellectual life in France in a manner that came to resemble the controversy over positivism in Germany. It was carried on in a civilized manner. Lévi-Strauss had in fact responded favorably to Ricoeur's critical characterization of structuralism as a type of Kantianism without a transcendental subject. Yet the publication of Ricoeur's comprehensive analysis of Freud, *De l'interprétation,* in 1965, met with a very different response.[3] Having lived through the poststructuralist dissolution of boundaries, it is almost impossible to imagine the scientistic ambition characteristic of early structuralism. To the youngsters in its thrall, Ricoeur, along with phenomenology and hermeneutics, seemed ridiculously unscientific and antiquated. The most furious reaction to Ricoeur's interpretation of Freud came from Jacques Lacan, some of whose seminars Ricoeur had attended. He disputed the unanalyzed Ricoeur's right to speak with authority about Freud, accused him of plagiarism, ridiculed him in front of his supporters, and broke off contact with him. In a climate characterized by Lacan's structuralist psychoanalysis and Althusser's structuralist Marxism, Ricoeur was bound to appear a hopeless outsider. His undisguised loyalty to the Christian faith made matters worse. Though Ricoeur had always gone out of his way to design his philosophical arguments such that others might agree with them regardless of religious motives, and as seriously as he of all people had taken the motives underlying the critiques of religion produced by Freud, Marx, and Nietzsche, he was now battered by the wanton scientism and the general aggressive lack of understanding that characterized the enthusiastic secularism of the late 1960s, in France and beyond. Then there was university politics itself. Ricoeur left the Sorbonne in the mid-1960s for the new university of Nanterre in the suburbs of Paris, where he hoped to play a leading role in the reform of the "mass university." In 1970, Maoist students, whose methods were modeled on those of the Chinese "Cultural Revolution," physically attacked him there. Later, as another crisis reached its peak, he called in the police to the campus. Some branded him a traitor for this, and, for others, the assault on him made him a laughing stock. The "martyr of a new political culture," in Alain Touraine's words, Ricoeur resigned from his offices and largely withdrew from French public life.

After a period of semi-exile at the Husserl Archive in Leuven, Ricoeur got a call from the University of Chicago. He was offered a post in the Divinity School as successor to the great Protestant theologian Paul Tillich as well as membership of the Committee on Social Thought. This call, Ricoeur believed with hindsight, saved his life intellectually and perhaps even physically. The atmosphere in Chicago was less politically heated than that in Paris; phenomenology and hermeneutics were not considered outmoded but were, in fact, attracting growing interest, and religious motives were not seen as reactionary esotericism. In fact, his friendship with Mircea Eliade, who had moved from Paris to Chicago some time before, intensified Ricoeur's interest in the scientific study of myth and religion. Above all, in characteristic fashion, Ricoeur again took the philosophical approach of articulating his own motives in new ways, and thereby transforming them, by opening oneself to another. From the start of his time teaching in Chicago, Ricoeur entered into a dialogue with analytical philosophy, which largely defines professional philosophy in the United States. The fruits of this new opening are apparent in the major works that Ricoeur published from the 1980s on.

In Ricoeur's three-volume study *Time and Narrative*,[4] an intellectual project rooted in Husserl's phenomenology of temporal consciousness and developed further by grappling with Heidegger, is now unmistakably articulated on the foundation provided by the analytical philosophy of history and narrative as immanent means of overcoming the "nomological" model in the discipline of history. But this study is even more broadly based in that Ricoeur deals authoritatively not only with "continental" and "analytical" philosophy but also with literary theory and "narrative semiotics," the philosophy of Aristotle and Augustine and the interpretation of literary works by Virginia Woolf, Thomas Mann, and Marcel Proust. Ricoeur is a thinker of sound judgment and tremendous breadth of vision. By comparing the narrative produced by the writer of history with literary fiction, he neither ignores the constructed character of the historical narrative nor does he annul its specific relationship with truth. The academic community has yet to fully understand this work's relevance to a vast range of subjects. Among its most impressive features is the concluding outline of a hermeneutics of historical consciousness, which follows a penetrating analysis of the "Hegelian temptation":

> Having left Hegel behind, can we still claim to think about history and the time of history? The answer would be negative if the idea of a "total mediation" were to exhaust the field of thought. But

another way remains, that of an open-ended, incomplete, imperfect mediation, namely, the network of interweaving perspectives of the expectation of the future, the reception of the past, and the experience of the present, with no *Aufhebung* into a totality where reason in history and its reality would coincide.[5]

This productive approach to the "Hegelian temptation" also points us toward the constitution of temporal consciousness through present action and to the role of narrative in the constitution of personal identity. As far as I can see, theology and literary theory have thus far paid greater heed to the potential of Ricoeur's work than the social sciences have—despite the fact that he deals with basic categories of social scientific thought. Ricoeur himself comprehensively developed the reflections on "narrative identity" present in embryonic form at the end of *Time and Narrative* in his major late work mentioned previously, *Oneself As Another.* This book, like so many important books before it, which explore the potential for faith in modern-day culture in the broadest sense, by thinkers ranging from William James through John Dewey and Alfred Whitehead to Charles Taylor, emerged from the Gifford Lectures at the University of Edinburgh. Characteristically, in the resulting book, Ricoeur did not include the last two of these lectures, which extended his line of thought into biblical hermeneutics. The main reason for this decision was his "concern to pursue, to the very last line, an autonomous, philosophical discourse."[6] He wants all his arguments—even if he himself developed them on the basis of faith in the Bible—either to convince the reader or to be rejected by him, but not because of belief in, or rejection of, such faith.

In this book, it is speech act theory and analytical action theory that serve Ricoeur as media for rearticulating his ideas. His distinction between the two meanings of identity, "mêmeté" and "ipséité ("sameness" and "selfness"), that is, mere identifiability as the same person over time and a self-created continuity despite changes—this alone would have been an excellent way of bringing order to a field of debate chronically plagued by conceptual obscurity. But for Ricoeur, this distinction is only a step toward linking what he has conceptually distinguished through a "dialectics of the person": "[T]he narrative operation has developed an entirely original concept of dynamic identity which reconciles the same categories that Locke took as contraries: identity and diversity."[7]

This book, too, features movement. Just as *Time and Narrative* guided us from poetological and methodological issues to the concept of narrative identity, *Oneself As Another* takes us beyond the development of the concept of narrative identity to generate an ethics. If the self is ultimately constituted in narrative form, its relationship to moral norms must also be embedded in this narrative structure. But Ricoeur, unlike Alasdair MacIntyre in his influential book *After Virtue*, refuses to allow this insight to tempt him into opposing a universalist concept of morality. Rather, he attempts to think about the pursuit of the Good Life together with the other and to the other's benefit in the framework of just institutions. More consistently than any other contemporary thinker, but most clearly prefigured in my opinion in classical U.S. pragmatism, Ricoeur synthesizes Aristotelianism and Kantianism in the field of ethics. Had it been paid greater heed, this work might have provided a way out of the impasses typical of the debates within moral philosophy on liberalism and communitarianism.

Ricoeur continued to be productive in his later years, until his death in 2005. In other texts, perhaps most eloquently in his speech on "Love and Justice" delivered at the University of Tübingen,[8] he set out his vision of extending a moral theory centered on justice and countering the tendency to lapse into mere utilitarian reciprocity. Another substantial work appeared in 2000: *La mémoire, l'histoire, l'oubli* fuses a phenomenology of remembering with a methodology of history and a hermeneutics of promising and forgiving, the crucial means of preventing the passing-by of time and of making a fresh start.[9]

Like all hermeneutical thinkers, Paul Ricoeur had to battle against the prejudice that he was more an interpreter and exegete than creative thinker. This prejudice applies even more to those who, like Ricoeur, have in fact painstakingly shown which of their predecessors had similar ideas and who stimulated their reflections. All his life, Ricoeur refused to adopt the habitus of the genius or to stage-manage his public persona by producing crass theses. He was a theoretical mediator who instinctively assumed the existence of a relative truth on either side of intense controversies and who attempted to integrate this into a synthesizing approach. He also steered clear of the perpetually admonitory air of "J'accuse" typical of politicizing intellectuals—while not hesitating to pen political essays, which accompanied his work through the decades. In terms of capacity for synthesis, originality, attachment to tradition, and openness to new ideas, his achievement resembles that of Jürgen Habermas in Germany. Ricoeur has not penetrated the professional world of the social sciences other than history to the same extent as Habermas. But he did more to consistently relate his philosophical work to biblical exegesis and reflection upon the Christian faith.[10]

Ricoeur persistently explored the relationship between religious experience and religious language, which is particularly interesting within the context of the present work. How, one is bound to ask, can the prelinguistic impact of these experiences be rendered communicable and integrated into the interpretive schemata of everyday life? Or are such experiences in fact only the expression of expectations preformed or determined by language and culture?

Paul Ricoeur grapples with this issue at various points in his oeuvre. Let us first consider the first of those two Gifford Lectures, which he famously refrained from incorporating into the book *Oneself As Another* in order, as he puts it, to avoid arousing suspicions of "crypto-theology" among philosophers. The text was published elsewhere under the title "Expérience et langage dans le discours religieux" ("Experience and language in religious discourse").[11] In this essay, Ricoeur first examines the obstacles lying in the way of a phenomenology of religion. He does not see these obstacles as primarily revolving around the fact that the phenomenological concept of intentionality entails an element of subjective usurpation vis-à-vis phenomena, which must inevitably conflict with the character of religion as an insight into the dependency of all subjectivity on something higher. Phenomenology, he asserts, has certainly developed the capacity to reconstruct experiences in which the subject becomes receptive to this radically other ("une altérité intégrale"); immediately subsequent to this argument, in the outlines of a "phenomenology of prayer," Ricoeur shows how this process of opening up to the Divine itself can again be turned into an active process. Ricoeur, in fact, sees the problematic nature of the linguistic communication of experiences of this kind, which appear to us to be the epitome of a state in which our entire person is directly affected, as the key problem facing any phenomenology of religion. Here again, he concedes that phenomenology is well past the stage in which it understood language merely as an unproductive additional layer above the truly substantial layer of experienced meanings, but this very insight, as he puts it, "damns phenomenology to pass through the Caudine yoke of a hermeneutics, and indeed more precisely a hermeneutics of texts or scripture."[12] He goes on to demonstrate that even the most intense religious experiences are mediated by culture, by showing how ideas of the immanence or transcendence of the Divine, its personal or anonymous character, the individualistic or "communitarian" orientation of faith, activism or passivism affect the interpretation of such experiences. For Ricoeur, this means that a true phenomenology of religion as such is an impossibility; all we can aspire to do is trace hermeneutically the broad outlines of an individual, specific religion, and on this basis apply the insights gained to other specific religions with a view to verifying them. This would be done on a comparative basis and in the spirit of a "hospitalité interreligieuse," an "interreligious hospitality." For the Christian tradition or perhaps for all religions based on a "holy scripture," thus for Judaism and Islam as well, Ricoeur himself brings out the hermeneutic interplay of the Word of God and sacred text, text and interpretive community, interpretive tradition and each new concrete expression thereof (or "minituarization," as Ricoeur puts it) in a given situation.

His subsequent comments show with tremendous sensitivity how religious self-discovery is possible through the reading of the sacred text, how the book becomes a mirror for the reader. I have no doubt that this is possible, and it is obvious that Ricoeur himself is speaking here on the basis of his own intense experience, which he manages to convey in his works of biblical hermeneutics.[13]

But I am irritated by one of the steps in his argument, a "non sequitur," which is surprising coming from a writer as careful as Ricoeur and which points to something deeper. Although I have no objection to the argument that the phenomenology of religion can only be a hermeneutic endeavor, I do not understand why such a hermeneutics should first and foremost be a hermeneutics of sacred texts rather than a hermeneutics of texts about religious experience. It might even be a rash move to talk of a hermeneutics of texts here, because this very quickly cuts out the interpretation of nonlinguistic articulations of religious experiences. But what seems to me more important systematically and more urgent in light of modern-day religious conditions is to distinguish clearly between a religious experience that is, as it were, established through the process of exegesis, and a religious experience in search of adequate articulation, however strongly experience and articulation might be influenced by the content of the text-based tradition.

More than eighty years before Ricoeur, another man gave the famous Gifford Lectures, and he had chosen precisely the path that I am calling for here. The empirical basis of William James's book *The Varieties of Religious Experience*[14] comprised autobiographical texts—texts by religious virtuosos, such as saints and founders of religions, but also by people like you and me, in which they speak of conversion and loss of faith, experiences with prayer, and mysticism. James's book, whose origins lie not in the philosophical school of phenomenology but in that of pragmatism, has been described as a better phenomenology of religion than many works claiming that very title.[15] Furthermore, the study of autobiographical narratives of religious experiences chimes perfectly with Ricoeur's emphasis on the formation of identity through narrative. The more individuals follow their own unique paths in the construction of religious meaning, the greater the need for us to approach the experiences they have along the way. The model privileged by Ricoeur, meanwhile, assumes that the study of the Holy Scripture is central to the religious life of individuals and communities, though this surely applies to a fairly small number of people nowadays. Furthermore, even for those who are very familiar with the practice of reading the Bible, it sounds a little like the notion of *sola scriptura*, the Protestant privileging of exegesis as opposed to all other sources of religious experience.

Yet a text by Ricoeur dating from 1974, *Manifestation et Proclamation,* went much farther.[16] The aim of this text is none other than to mediate between a hermeneutics of proclamation and a phenomenology of the manifestation of the sacred. Here, the key authors upon whom he draws in producing his phenomenology of the sacred are Rudolf Otto and especially Mircea Eliade, but not, once again, William James. Once again, this decision has far-reaching consequences: From the very outset, Ricoeur's sights are set on a phenomenology of the sacred, but not a phenomenology of religious experience or of the experience of the sacred. Unlike James (and Émile Durkheim), for whom no inherent relationship exists between the quality of objects and their sacredness, Otto and Eliade insisted on describing the numinous as a quality innate to objects themselves. This was a strength, in that it brought a whole range of specific issues of interest to scholars of religion into the equation, but also a weakness, in that it tended to push into the background the power of sacredness, with which every phenomenon is potentially saturated.

In the previously mentioned text, clearly influenced by Eliade, his colleague at Chicago for many years, Ricoeur brings out how little the experience of the sacred itself is linguistically constituted and language-centered in many religions. Of course, Ricoeur explains, there is a connection between the manifestations of the sacred and the myth—and thus a discursive account of the sacred. But this, he tells us, takes us no further than a kind of minimalist hermeneutics. Here, sacredness substantiates discursiveness, and not the other way around. Unlike Eliade, Ricoeur does not incorporate this hermeneutics of proclamation into a phenomenology of the sacred, which is concerned in the main with primitive religions and "nonliterate religions" (rather than the religious experience of the modern person), but deploys it to counter this mere phenomenology. This he does primarily by interpreting the Old Testament prophets as radically antimagic, "desacralizing" actors who help the Word gain the upper hand over the numinous. Ricoeur's view of ancient Judaism thus strongly resembles that of Max Weber. It is, however, susceptible to the same criticisms made of Weber, who was accused of projecting Protestantism backward onto ancient Judaism. But Ricoeur certainly opposes Rudolf Bultmann and Dietrich Bonhoeffer, who take this line of thought too far. Ricoeur, the great theoretical mediator, aims to mediate between manifestation and proclamation. From this perspective, the Word is not only the overcoming of the merely numinous but its transformation. Particularly through the sacraments, the (primitive) sacred ritual is transformed into a symbolic representation of *Heilsgeschichte,* the history of salvation. But without such sacredness, Ricoeur concludes, the Word itself becomes abstract and intellectualist.

I agree with this unreservedly. The older text emerges as less language-centered than its newer counterpart. At the very least, it opens up a text-centered understanding of religious experience to sacramental experiences. Robert Bellah, the great American sociologist of religion, would see this as a case of Word-centered Protestantism moving somewhat closer to Catholicism, which he considers an appropriate response to a certain contemporary Protestantization of Catholicism resulting from the increasing affirmation of religious individualization.[17] But I would wish to go even further and open up the sphere of present-day religious experience to an even greater extent in order, by confronting the full range of these phenomena in unprejudiced fashion, to advocate Christianity as a language for the articulation of these experiences.

NOTES

1. Paul Ricoeur, *Oneself As Another,* trans. Kathleen Blamey (Chicago: University of Chicago Press, 1996). Originally published as *Soi-même comme un autre* (Paris: Seuil, 1990).

2. François Dosse, *Paul Ricoeur. Les sens d'une vie* (Paris: La Découverte, 1997). I have drawn mainly on this work and Ricoeur's intellectual autobiography *Réflexion faite* (Paris: Esprit, 1995) for the biographical information, as well as François Dosse, *History of Structuralism,* 2 vols. (Minneapolis: University of Minnesota Press, 1999). Originally published as *Histoire du structuralisme* (Paris: La Découverte, 1991); Dosse, *L'empire du sens. L'humanisation des sciences humaines* (Paris: La Découverte, 1995). English translation: *Empire of Meaning: The Humanization of the Social Sciences* (Minneapolis: University of Minnesota Press, 1999).

3. Paul Ricoeur, *Freud and Philosophy: An Essay on Interpretation* (New Haven, CT: Yale University Press, 1970). Originally published as *De l'interprétation: essai sur Freud* (Paris: Seuil, 1965).

4. Paul Ricoeur, *Time and Narrative,* 3 vols., trans. Kathleen McLaughlin and David Pellauer (Chicago: University of Chicago Press, 1984–1988). Originally published in French between 1983 and 1985.

5. Ibid., vol. 3, 207.

6. *Oneself As Another,* 24.

7. Ibid., 143.

8. Paul Ricoeur, "Love and Justice," in *Figuring the Sacred: Religion, Narrative, and Imagination* (Minneapolis: Fortress Press, 1995), 315–329.

9. Paul Ricoeur, *La mémoire, l'histoire, l'oubli* (Paris: Seuil, 2000); English translation: *Memory, History, Forgetting* (Chicago: University of Chicago Press, 2004). *Le parcours de la reconnaissance* (Paris: Stock, 2004); English translation: *The Course of Recognition* (Cambridge, MA: Harvard University Press, 2005).

10. Bernhard Waldenfels has long led the field in bringing Ricoeur to a German audience. See Waldenfels, *Phänomenologie in Frankreich* (Frankfurt am Main: Suhrkamp, 1983), 266–335. German authors, mostly of a younger generation, have engaged productively with Ricoeur's philosophy in two recent anthologies: Burkhard Liebsch, ed., *Hermeneutik des Selbst—Im Zeichen des Anderen* (Freiburg and Munich: Alber, 1999); Andris Breitling, Stefan Orth, and Birgit Schaaff, eds., *Das herausgeforderte Selbst. Perspektiven auf Paul Ricoeurs Ethik* (Würzburg: Königshausen und Neumann, 1999).

11. Paul Ricoeur, "Expérience et langage dans le discours religieux," in Jean-François Courtine et al., *Phénoménologie et théologie* (Paris: Criterion, 1992), 15–39.

12. Ibid., 19; (translation by the present author).

13. See, for example, Paul Ricoeur and André LaCocque, *Penser la bible* (Paris: Seuil, 1998).

14. William James, *The Varieties of Religious Experience* (Cambridge, MA: Harvard University Press, 1985).

15. James M. Edie, *William James and Phenomenology* (Bloomington: Indiana University Press, 1987), 49ff.

16. Paul Ricoeur, "Manifestation et Proclamation," *Archivio di Filosofia* 44 (1974): 2–3, 57–76. English translation in *Figuring the Sacred: Religion, Narrative, and Imagination* (Minneapolis: Fortress Press, 1995), 48–67.

17. Robert Bellah, "Flaws in the Protestant Code: Some Religious Sources of America's Troubles," *Ethical Perspectives* 7 (2000): 288–299.

8

Post-Secular Religion?
On Jürgen Habermas

German public opinion was unanimous in regarding Jürgen Habermas's October 2001 Peace Prize acceptance speech as a sensation.[1] Commentators in the culture sections of newspapers went as far as to declare the speech "epoch-making"; the reaction of many of those in the audience at the Paulskirche in Frankfurt, that famous place in German history, or watching on television, resembled a religious awakening. What had happened, and what does this event tell us about the relationship between religion and politics today?

Without doubt, as so often in his life, Habermas's sure instincts had enabled him to build a bridge between his systematic thought and current events. He not only managed to satisfy the general hunger for interpretation of a public stirred up by the events of September 11, 2001, he also offered a way out, particularly to all those liberally inclined intellectuals who had long harbored the happy notion that secularization is a quasi-automatic feature of modernization—and whose conviction had now suffered a serious blow. For them, he built into his exposition the rousing new concept of the "post-secular" society. And for believers and the churches, like his book on bioethics, his speech represented a generous offer to engage in dialogue. Because it came from the so-called heir of the mythical Frankfurt School, the most effective prophet of the incomplete project of Enlightenment, they were also bound to welcome it with open arms; after all, at the very least it opened up an opportunity for territorial expansion. Nonetheless, it would be going too far at this stage to welcome Habermas back to Christianity as a prodigal son.

However, viewed with a degree of distance, neither Habermas's diagnosis, nor his offer of dialogue, are entirely free of deficiencies. After all, the term *post-secular,* if it is to be meaningful, must refer to a change vis-à-vis an earlier phase. But it is not clear when this earlier *secular* society is supposed to have existed and what one can actually mean by the term. It is true that such lack of clarity has failed to prevent the lively circulation of other "posts"; but particularly in the case of such a notoriously ambiguous term as *secularization,* it is worthwhile taking a closer look. It might refer to religion's loss of significance but also to the emergence of modern, religiously neutralized statehood. By no means do these always coincide. From a global perspective, it would be quite wrong to suggest that religion is declining in importance. Despite the further spread of industrialization, urbanization, and education over the past few decades, all world religions have retained or increased their vitality. The key exceptions are well known: In some communist countries the totalitarian suppression of religious life was successful, and the consequences persist to this day; across large parts of Western Europe and in some ex-colonial settler societies (such as New Zealand and Argentina), at least since the 1960s, there has been a long, drawn out, creeping, and unforced decline in religious commitment. But it would be utterly Eurocentric to conclude that these facts constitute a global trend. This claim cannot even be applied to all European societies; it fails spectacularly in the case of the United States. That country is in many ways deceptively similar to Europe, but in religious terms, it is another world from, for example, modern Germany. Again and again, therefore, attempts have been made to exoticize the United States as a special case and to trace its religious vitality back to the history of its foundation. Yet these explanations fail to shed light on why religiosity in the United States only truly flourished after the state was founded at the end of the eighteenth century. From the perspective of contemporary modernization across the globe, it is Europe rather than the United States that seems the exception.

But if the assumption that modernization necessarily leads to the retreat of religions is losing its plausibility, the term *post-secular,* together with the notion that Islam is out of sync with technological advances, is also beginning to look shaky. *Post-secular* now expresses not a sudden increase in religiosity following its epoch-making decline—but rather a shift in the consciousness of those who had felt justified in regarding religions as moribund. For Habermas, a society that "adapts to the fact that religious communities continue to exist in a context of ongoing secularization" is *post-secular.* But who exactly had failed to adapt to this continued existence? It would perhaps have been better to admit in self-critical fashion that one had underestimated religion—rather than dressing one's mistake up in a term redolent of epochal change. Habermas was certainly not alone in underestimating religion. However much he might have striven to maintain a distance from utopianism, it was precisely the tremendous pretensions of his communicative understanding of rationality that many found so electrifying about his writings. If he saw the authority of the sacred gradually passing to whatever consensus was considered justified at a given time through a process of "linguistification of the sacred,"[2] one could take this to mean that all the functions of religion would be taken over entirely by processes of rational agreement. Many "secular" intellectuals continue to cling to this vision even at a time when Habermas himself seems far from convinced of it. The Enlightenment, or Nietzschean, overtones of "God is dead," almost a matter of good form in the academic world, have practically disappeared from his work. The more we ascribe merely weak motivational power to any consensus amenable to rational generation, the more vital it is to look into sources of greater moral motivation and more intensive human commitment.

The second possible meaning of secularization comes into play here. This spotlights not the decline of religion but the restrictions put on its potential impact in a secularized, that is, religiously neutralized, state. Here, *post-secular* does not mean that religion is becoming increasingly important or that people have begun to pay it more attention but that the secular state or the public has changed its attitude toward the continued existence of religious communities and the ideas generated by them. Once again, though, the question is whether *post-secular* is the right word for such a transformation. It is not the secular state that is being overcome but merely a secularist self-image. And again, we might ask to whom such a self-image in fact applied. The controversy surrounding the German Federal Constitutional Court's ruling on crucifixes just a few years ago showed very clearly how greatly the ideas of the general population, politicians, and constitutional jurisprudence differ. Some saw the ruling as establishing a liberal principle that should have been taken for granted long before and welcomed it as a facet of the Westernization of the Federal Republic of Germany. But this is to forget that, particularly in the West, however separate state and church might be, a question mark always hangs over exactly where the dividing line lies. Informed by debates on bioethics, Habermas himself now frames his arguments in far more subtle terms—and it is remarkable just how much his transformation seems once again to articulate a more general shift in consciousness. He counters a modernism lacking all appreciation for the profound meaning of the Judeo-Christian tradition, or that simply declares it null and void, with the notion of a secularization that is able to "salvage" this meaning. His role model is Immanuel Kant. Just as Kant did not reject the moral content of the Christian tradition but rather attempted to translate it into a philosophical language that might meet with the approval even of those who do not share the religious presuppositions, many people now wish to rescue the ideas embedded in the Judeo-Christian heritage, such as the notion that man is made in God's image and that we are the children of God, from the dangers of the unlimited disposability of the person.

But the problem of this translation and the notion of a "salvaging" secularization can appear new only to those for whom it has not always determined everyday life, as it has for religious people. What is astonishing, and profoundly significant, is that so many people found Habermas's plea sensational. Because it is impossible in a secularized public sphere to draw directly on religious convictions to develop one's arguments, Christians and other religious people have, since the establishment of a religiously neutralized public sphere, always been confronted with the problem of avoiding ghettoization, even at the level of language, and of expressing their convictions in languages other than the traditionally religious.[3] Only fundamentalists of all stripes refuse to accept this situation and see the pressure to translate traditional beliefs to which this situation gives rise as being itself illegitimate; this is nothing less than the definition of fundamentalism. Habermas's call for a "salvaging"—rather than destructive—secularization explicitly acknowledges this. It is an eloquent plea to the secular camp to go further in acknowledging the daily translation that believers have to perform and to reciprocate.

Yet the underlying assumption that there is a dichotomous alternative in the evaluation of secularization is misleading. It is not simply an opposition between those who welcomed secularization as "the successful *taming* of clerical authority" by secular authorities because "religious ways of thinking and forms of life are *replaced* by rational, in any case superior, equivalents" (Habermas), and those who could see only degeneracy and illegal expropriation in the same process. For the history of the West features many examples of religiously motivated struggles for the freedom of the individual, and thus for the taming of state and ecclesiastical authority, which do *not,* however, aim to *replace* religious ways of thinking and ways of life but rather to *individualize* them. It is one thing to concede the religious roots of the Western legal tradition and its moral underpinnings, quite another to recognize how religious forces have driven even the establishment of religious freedom and individual rights to liberty. Should this fail to be recognized, religion appears as nothing more than an aspect of cultural heritage that should not be forgotten or as a relic—if it is not perceived as an outright threat to a liberal order—but it is certainly not regarded as a living presence.

Historically speaking, however, this would be a very inadequate notion. To be sure, history features examples of religious tolerance under quite different regimes and in very different forms. For the most part, it was based—in the spirit of enlightened absolutism in the Prussia of Frederick the Great or within a Catholic framework in colonial Maryland, for example—on straightforward calculations of utility. Far more interesting are cases in which the powers that be not only refrain from violently enforcing the truths of their own faith but also encourage religious tolerance on the basis of (often religious) values themselves. This presupposes the conviction that faith forced upon one is not worthy of the name and that I must therefore want freedom from state paternalism not only as concerns my own faith but for everyone: Roger Williams wished to establish this freedom of religion not only for Christians of all kinds but also "for Jews, heathens and Turks" when he left Massachusetts in 1636 and founded a community in the colony of Rhode Island, where for the first time in history the religious freedom of each individual was guaranteed.[4] And it was not only this establishment of religious freedom that was driven by religious enthusiasm. The articulation of human rights in the eighteenth century or the struggle to abolish slavery in the nineteenth century were by no means—as much of the liberal and Enlightenment mythology would have it—solely the result of Enlightenment ideas. The precise nature of the relationship between religious motives, in North America, for example, and antireligious notions that sacralize

reason itself, in France, for instance, is certainly complex and contested—but it is clear that at many of the key junctions in the modern
history of freedom, it was fought for not in the face of religion but
by religion. And this becomes even more plausible if we include the
religiously motivated resistance to the tyrannies of the secular ersatz
religions of the twentieth century.

In his speech at the Paulskirche, Habermas actually went beyond
those liberal thinkers for whom all substantial values appear as threats
to domestic peace and who therefore push for the public sphere to be
emptied of religious symbols, the establishment of a laicist hegemony
and public agreement on matters of values only in the sense of a
minimal consensus. Richard Rorty, for example, has championed this
conception in particularly crass fashion most recently, and surprisingly
to many people in Germany, in his speech of thanks for (of all things)
the Meister Eckhart Prize. After all, most friends of Rorty's postmodern
version of pragmatism had previously been entirely unaware that his
plea for playful conversation and an ironic art of living conceal an
outright militant "anticlericalism" and a quasi-positivistic conception
of historical stages, according to which the religious and metaphysical
stages are being replaced by a new age, but of literature rather than
science. Such a "view, that Church institutions, however much good
they might do, still endanger the wellbeing of democratic societies"
and that therefore "institutionalized religion [must] finally [disappear]
from the scene,"[5] can be countered by the idea of a plural public sphere
energized by its very plurality, of a mutually tolerant dialogue that
must be permanently maintained between believers and nonbelievers,
and of a serious effort to come to an understanding about values by
learning from each other, an understanding that would be far more
than a lowest common denominator. But this should not occur solely
as a gesture of goodwill toward religious perspectives. It seems even
more important to give institutional shape to the task of constantly
reestablishing the boundaries between secular and religious reasons,
between ethics and politics. We must ensure that there is space for this
dialogue in politics, at the margins of politics (in church forums, for
example), and in the educational system. But this insight must also
help guarantee the general institutional conditions for the survival of
religious communities.

Traditionally, the Federal Republic of Germany has done a rea-
sonably good job of guaranteeing these conditions. In recent years,
however, in the context of the ruling on crucifixes and the religious

education debate, the regulations governing the running of businesses on Sundays and public holidays and the issue of bioethics, these guarantees have been weakened. How ironic it is that as we become more aware how well founded these guarantees are, some commentators declare that this entails the emergence of something new, namely, post-secular society, rather than the preservation of something old. This "novelty" is not new, but the old arrangement is both venerable and valuable.

NOTES

1. Jürgen Habermas, "Faith and Knowledge," in *The Future of Human Nature* (Cambridge: Polity Press, 2003), 101–115.
2. Jürgen Habermas, *The Theory of Communicative Action*, vol. 2, trans. Thomas McCarthy (Boston: Beacon; Cambridge: Polity, 1987).
3. See Hans Joas, ed., *Was sind religiöse Überzeugungen?* (Göttingen: Wallstein, 2003).
4. More detail can be found in Hans Joas, "Max Weber and the Origin of Human Rights: A Study of Cultural Innovation," in Charles Camic et al., eds., *Max Weber's "Economy and Society": A Critical Companion* (Stanford, CA: Stanford University Press, 2005), 366–382. For a comprehensive treatment, see Perez Zagorin, *How the Idea of Religious Toleration Came to the West* (Princeton, NJ: Princeton University Press, 2003).
5. Richard Rorty, "Korinther 13 und die Schlachtbank der Geschichte," *Süddeutsche Zeitung*, December 4, 2001.

PART 3

Human Dignity

9

Decency, Justice, Dignity: On Avishai Margalit

How can a politics be established whose guiding value is the dignity of every human being? Originally in Hebrew, Avishai Margalit's *The Decent Society* enjoyed tremendous international success as soon as its English translation appeared.[1] Reviewers were almost unanimously positive, several ranking it alongside John Rawls's *A Theory of Justice*, published in 1971, in importance; for a new book in the field of moral philosophy and normative political theory, there could hardly be higher praise. The following critical reflections are not intended to deny the brilliance of Margalit's work but to open up a dialogue between ways of thinking that overlap in part, but that also differ markedly. After briefly discussing some difficulties in Margalit's philosophy concerning the relationship between "decency" and "justice," I scrutinize whether Margalit's proposed approach to the justification of values is convincing or whether we should look for a superior alternative.

My point of departure is the question of the precise relationship between Margalit's guiding ideal of decency and Rawls's emphasis on justice as the most important value in constructing a political order. At least at the beginning of Margalit's book, most readers are likely to gain the impression that, according to Margalit, decency is a more modest ideal than justice and that *The Decent Society* is a far less ambitious project than Rawls's *A Theory of Justice*. There are numerous passages in the book in which the author himself discusses the relationship between the two ideals in terms of a hierarchy of values or a lexicographical order. If we assume that these passages are correct, then clearly the decent society is not necessarily a just society, but the just society must be a decent society. Some of the most thorough and sympathetic reviewers obviously came away with the same impression. Alan Wolfe, for example, called Margalit's book a "softening of the Rawlsian project," and the ideal of decency a "toned-down version" of the ideal of justice.[2] This interpretation is confirmed when Margalit extends his hierarchy of political ideals, elaborating that the avoidance of physical cruelty would be a still more modest ideal than the avoidance of humiliation in the decent society or, as we have seen, the avoidance of injustice in a just society. Margalit provides some additional reflections on so-called second-bests, but these are minor modifications only, merely relating to our ideas about how to attain more modest ideals. Although it is for the most part easier to achieve more modest goals, it might be necessary to opt for an altogether different strategy in order to do so—different from that which one would have pursued had one had the more ambitious ideal in mind. The order of ideals in a hierarchy of values cannot always be translated directly into a sequence of steps within a dynamic strategy of action.

Everything, therefore, seems clarified and settled—until the reader reaches the final chapter. Here she may, with some surprise, encounter a passage in which the author declares that a just society is necessarily a decent society—at least if this just society chimes with Rawls's definition—but that within the framework of Rawls's theory of justice, this point is difficult to prove. "The idea is that if a theory with 'Kantian' sensitivity to human dignity such as Rawls's is liable to encounter difficulties in reconciling the just and the decent society, then the relation between the two types of society is less clear than it might seem" (272). The most striking examples of such complications are cases of action geared toward justice—the distribution of goods being an example—which humiliate the recipients. "The people distributing the goods may act in a humiliating way even if the end result is the best possible distribution of the goods" (280). At least one of the earlier chapters points in the same direction, namely, that which scrutinizes citizenship, particularly its symbolic dimensions. Here, Margalit's reflections remind the reader of the communitarian critiques of individualist liberalism and thus of a type of thinking that claims that justice is not necessarily the only or most worthy ideal for a social order. In his direct confrontation with Rawls, Margalit brings up several other confusing points.[3] First, he distinguishes between the letter and the spirit of Rawls's work and takes exception to the former rather than the latter for ignoring the relationship between justice and decency. Well, one might object here, nobody is perfect, and a lack of clarity in Rawls reveals nothing about the systematic relationship between the two ideals. Second, Margalit criticizes Rawls for ignoring nonmembers and the issue of access to membership in his theory of justice. "In order to assess whether a Rawlsian just society is also decent, it must therefore be judged by its treatment of people who are dependent on its institutions even if they are not members, such as foreign workers (*Gastarbeiter*), who do the dirty work in developed countries without being citizens there" (274–275). I think this is a misunderstanding: Rawls's membership is not defined in the legal terms of citizenship but in the action-theoretical way familiar from John Dewey's *The Public and Its Problems*,[4] as the collectivity of all those affected by certain actions. But however we might interpret the ins and outs of Rawls, we are clearly confronted with a quite different claim here, namely, that we can conceive of societies that are just but not decent. Decency might then be a higher ideal than justice. This is the conclusion drawn by all those (like Axel Honneth)[5] who anchor an emphatic notion of decency in the ideal of universal mutual recognition. In her review of Margalit's book, German political scientist Gesine Schwan[6] puts it in the following way: A decent society is simultaneously more and less than a just society. From a logical point of view, however, no object can be simultaneously more and less than a different object—unless we are referring to different aspects of it. This reviewer's paradoxical statement signals that we are dealing here not so much with an inconsistency in Margalit's work but with an issue whose need for resolution his text fails to acknowledge.

We might look for a route out of this dilemma by deciding not to see decency and justice in terms of a hierarchical order in the first place. I suggest that we view them as *competing* ideals. There are certain circumstances in which the two ideals are in harmony or provide each other with mutual support. But other circumstances exist in which they compete and are out of sync. As we have learned from Isaiah Berlin's "value pluralism," this is the normal state of affairs in the world of values.[7] Just as "justice" and "freedom" or "freedom" and "equality" might be easy or difficult to reconcile, depending on the situation, so "justice" and "decency" cannot always be placed within a clear hierarchical or sequential order. The tension between them forces us again and again to make difficult, risky, and perhaps tragic choices between them.

This is a far-from-comforting conclusion. But if it is true, we are immediately faced with further discomfort, because it forces us to open a Pandora's box of additional unwelcome conclusions. In Margalit's construction, the decent society is defined as the avoidance of institutional humiliation. The decent society is located higher on the hierarchy of values than a merely "bridled" society (147), which is defined by the avoidance of physical cruelty. For Margalit, the avoidance of cruelty is so basic that it requires no moral justification; it is the point where all moral justifiability ends. This conclusion has much to recommend it. It recalls Dostoevsky's pronouncement that a revolution cannot be justified if it claims the life of a single child. But if we assume that the two ideals can be in competition with each other, it is difficult to defend even this assumption. It suddenly becomes possible to imagine such an intolerable degree of injustice that countermeasures can be justified despite their indecent or perhaps even cruel consequences. This should not be misunderstood as a justification of violent social movements or a cynical "Realpolitik" that ignore or belittle the avoidance of humiliation or cruelty. I am merely pointing out that we have a problem here. How can we justify human dignity as an unconditional ideal existing *alongside* that of justice, if we cannot consider values to be arranged in a clearly hierarchical way and the fundamental value of cruelty avoidance cannot be conceived as the self-evident end of all efforts at justification? The following critical reflections are devoted to this problem of justification.

Margalit himself distinguishes between three different philosophical strategies in this regard. The so-called positive strategy attempts to identify properties common to all human beings as the basis for universal respect for human beings. The Christian notion of the soul clearly fulfilled such a function; Kant's philosophy, with its conception of the human being as a rational being capable of moral autonomy, offers the most influential attempt at a positive postmetaphysical justification. Jürgen Habermas—whom Margalit does not discuss—attempts to transform Kantian rationality into communicative rationality and thus to found universal human dignity in the quasi-transcendental conditions of human communication and interaction. But a religious justification cannot expect automatic acceptance in a partially secularized world, and the other positive justifications all suffer from their attribution to the human species of capacities not found in all individual human beings, at least not in an empirical sense. Although infants might be considered potential holders of these properties, the question remains of how we should conceptualize incurably mentally handicapped or senile people who, almost by definition, do not share the abilities or properties we have used to define humankind. A clear separation between empirical and transcendental[8] does not help us here, either, because it fails to resolve the question of why we should "frame" interactions transcendentally when it is obvious that this is not, or not fully, appropriate. Margalit experiments with his own idea of positive justification—the human ability to make a fresh start, to repent and reinvent oneself with the future in mind. But I believe that the criticisms directed against other accounts of typical human attributes, namely, that these cannot be applied to each individual human being, fatally undermines this proposal as well.

This thought experiment, however, is not the main thrust of Margalit's argument, which is to be found in a different strategy, namely, negative justification. This means justification of the value of dignity not by means of a list of positively given universal anthropological attributes but rather by means of an argument according to which humiliation is a violation of dignity. Here, Margalit follows Judith Shklar's and Richard Rorty's "liberalism of fear." But he is far from entirely consistent here. When he writes about punitive justice, for example, he states explicitly that the relevant institutions must be geared toward the positive value of human dignity. I do not consider these and similar passages mere lapses: One cannot help but switch back and forth between positive references to values and negative references to their absence, even if there might be strong moral, logical, or cognitive reasons to prefer the negative strategy of justification. When Margalit writes, in a particularly moving chapter about how humiliation, even in cases where other people are treated as nonhuman objects, presupposes the perception of the other as a human being, he comes close to the idea of performative self-contradiction so popular in the semiotically transformed transcendental philosophy of contemporary discourse ethics. I see two other main reasons why the strategy of negative justification fails to resolve the problem. Both stem from the fact that humiliation has an immanent relationship to reasons. Humiliation is not simply a psychological phenomenon, but is defined by Margalit as "any sort of behavior or condition that constitutes *a sound reason* for a person to consider his or her self-respect injured" (9). But who decides what "a sound reason" is: the instigator of the humiliation, the victim, or a neutral observer? I am not thinking of purely practical matters here. If "sound reasons" form part of the definition of humiliation, there must be cases in which people feel humiliated without such reasons and others in which they do not feel humiliated despite having reason to. A paranoid person who constantly feels humiliated by others is an example of the first type, and a mentally handicapped person or one in a coma are examples of the second. I do not dispute that "sound reasons" must feature in any definition of humiliation, but I would point out that this thwarts the strategy of negative justification. The avoidance of humiliation as a subjective fact does not constitute an absolute value if we introduce "sound reasons" into our definition. We would then refute some supposed feelings of humiliation as unfounded and would inevitably enter into a debate about what should count as a sound reason. Margalit writes of the moral legitimacy or illegitimacy of groups, but lacks explicit criteria for legitimacy. He calls those groups that do not humiliate their own members legitimate, but the question remains as to what, beyond subjective experience, the criteria for humiliation might be.

We are thus compelled to consider the third strategy, which Margalit mentions but fails to take very seriously. This he calls a "skeptical" strategy; he describes it as an attempt to take the cultural practice of respect as the starting point for justifying the value of dignity and decency. What he has in mind here is probably David Hume, as well as Richard Rorty's demonstration of a relaxed attitude toward questions of philosophical justification. Margalit finds this skeptical strategy insufficient or even dangerous: insufficient because it can only explicate an ideal inherent in a practice that already exists, and dangerous because it is unable to repudiate nihilist objections that the value of human dignity is just a remnant of an obsolete religious or political tradition devoid of all claim to ongoing validity. Margalit underestimates the potential of this type of thinking and is misled by the deficiencies in Rorty's particular version of anti-foundational-ism and pragmatism into believing that this version exhausts the full potential of such thinking.

First of all, it is wrong to call this strategy of justification "skep-tical," because its proponents are skeptical only with respect to the need for philosophical justification; they are not skeptical at all as regards the validity of the values in question. In this respect, they are perhaps the least skeptical of all because they take these values for granted and assume that they require no philosophical justification. I would call this strategy "nonfoundationalist" or, if you will, pragmatist. What does this strategy consist in? Negatively speaking, it keeps its distance from the business of philosophical justification. Why so? Because its proponents believe that an attachment to values is not the result of a completely or largely rational process. We develop our attachment to values in the processes of self-formation and, when the core structures of our identity have been established, in experiences of self-transcendence.[9] We have experiences in which something appears to us unquestionably good or bad, attractive or repellent, praiseworthy or outrageous. In most cases, rational justification is not the origin but the consequence of value commitments; we might be open to discussing the realization of our deepest values, but not these values themselves. They are deeply emotional, full of passion, and constitutive of our selves. This is neither the place to delineate the phenomenology of such experiences of self-transcendence in individual prayer or collective ecstasy, love and natural piety, conversations and moral feelings, nor the place to present the theoretical problems involved in the adequate conceptualization of terms such as *self* and *self-transcendence*.[10] But it is important to avoid the frequent misunderstanding that this approach is a complete irrationalism. If you accept for a moment my statements on the genesis of our value attachments as empirically true, you will see how this changes our view of what philosophical justification is and can be. Philosophical justification then emerges as an act in the empirical world—it is divested of some of its age-old prestige as a higher, extra-mundane activity. It is nothing other than an attempt to convince others to accept certain norms and values. I have no objection whatsoever to such attempts. But the foundationalist philosopher sees himself not as attempting to convince others empirically but as delivering a complete and ultimate justification and thus *compelling* others to accept his conclusions by the force of reason. Foundationalist philosophers justify their attempts at philosophical justification by pointing to the necessity of convincing others within one's own culture (such as neo-Nazis) or in a different culture (the Chinese communist government for instance) to accept certain values. Again, empirically I have grave doubts that these adversaries of the Western value tradition could ever be convinced by philosophical argument, and I doubt that foundationalist philosophers themselves believe that they could.

If this is the case, and if the necessity of convincing others was the main reason for choosing this approach, why not try a different one? This would involve reflecting on the experiences that inspired our value commitments and transferring one's understanding to a different culture. This would mean proposing new interpretations of experiences in other cultures or in our own and shifting constantly between such new interpretations and proposing new practices. This is not relativism fighting universalism—I am convinced that many experiences are anthropological universals. Cruelty and humiliation, for example, are often, though not always, immediately understandable in other cultures. But this approach takes cultural differences in the interpretation of experiences more seriously and gives up the dream of a justification independent of its context of origin.

To some, this approach may sound awfully Rortyan. It is not! The shortest and perhaps most elegant way to explain why it is not would be to say: It follows in the footsteps of William James, not Richard Rorty. It criticizes foundationalist philosophy not in the spirit of postmodern arbitrariness and playfulness but in order to open up a sphere in which we have a will or, to put it better, a right to believe—to believe in ultimate values that might, but need not to be, religious values. To me, foundationalist philosophy's attempt to justify ultimate values resembles attempts to prove the existence of God. But, as Kant and James have taught us,[11] the impossibility of proof is not the proof of impossibility. In the context of Margalit's philosophy of the decent society as one free of institutional humiliation, what I mean by this can best be illustrated by reference to the fate of the Christian concept of the soul. If the Christian notion of the soul is no longer immediately plausible, we need to reconstruct it in such a way that we do full justice to its original meaning. I know of no serious contemporary thinker who believes we can simply continue to understand the "soul" as the true core of every human being and the basis for universal human dignity in terms of a metaphysics of substance, whether in a pre-Cartesian or Cartesian sense as an immaterial substance in the world of matter. But I would argue that certain ways of thinking that claim to supersede this important intellectual tradition have also revealed their insufficiency. Post-Jamesian pragmatists like George Herbert Mead, Charles Horton Cooley, and John Dewey have clearly developed their theories of the self as an attempt to replace a substantialist understanding of the soul with a functionalist definition of the psychical and an intersubjectivist explanation of the constitution of the self.[12] But although this is an enormous achievement in the history of social psychology and sociology, it loses sight of another dimension of the older notion of the soul—namely, the sacred character of each human being, whether he has developed communicative and self-reflexive abilities or not. Nietzsche's postmetaphysical thinking is permeated by his passionate hatred of the Jewish and Christian traditions. I find a regrettably strong Nietzschean influence in Margalit's book. He not only accepts Nietzsche's understanding of resentment as a source of the value of "compassion" but also seems to follow Nietzsche in interpreting the Christian value of humility as servility. This is far from the truth. If I am right, the Christian value of humility is not a religious version of ancient Stoicism but an attempt to avoid a self-congratulatory attitude in moral matters, *superbia,* a pride in being morally superior to others. For a Christian, even acting morally and having self-respect has to be seen as a result of Divine love and grace—it is not worthless, according to the Christian tradition, but neither is it entirely one's own achievement; it must therefore be lived with humility.[13] Nietzsche never understood the Christian value of love, and this tainted all his contributions. My alternative approach involves following William James and Émile Durkheim—Durkheim with respect to the cultural genesis of new values, such as the sacredness of every person, and James with respect to the genesis of the individual attachment to old or new values.

This understanding of the genesis of values is in narrative form rather than that of an entirely rational argument. We can do no more than tell stories about the genesis of values. We can disseminate these stories and motivate others to listen to them—but stories will never take the form of full-blown philosophical justification. This applies to all *values* and all attempts to universalize values. My conception takes a different approach to *norms,* which, if I am right, are related to anthropologically universal structures of human action and coop- eration and which can be justified in fully rational terms as much as can cognitive validity claims.[14] But values are different. The value of justice has a special relationship to these norms. But as a value, it is on the same level as other values such as dignity and decency.[15] At least in a pragmatic sense, advancing our understanding of the genesis of values seems more urgent than philosophical justification—whether it pursues a positive or negative strategy.

NOTES

1. Avishai Margalit, *The Decent Society* (Cambridge, MA: Harvard University Press, 1996); subsequent page references in the text refer to this volume.

2. Alan Wolfe, "Before Justice," *The New Republic*, May 27, 1996, 33–36, esp. 34.

3. I examine only some of his points here.

4. John Dewey, *The Public and Its Problems* (New York: Holt, 1927).

5. Axel Honneth, "A Society Without Humiliation? On Avishai Margalit's Draft of a 'Decent Society,'" *European Journal of Philosophy* 5 (1997): 306–324.

6. Gesine Schwan, "Anständig, das ist mehr oder weniger als gerecht," *Süddeutsche Zeitung*, December 29, 1997.

7. John Gray's elaboration of value pluralism as the systematic core of Berlin's work is particularly persuasive: John Gray, *Isaiah Berlin* (Princeton, NJ: Princeton University Press, 1996). See also Hans Joas, "Value Pluralism and Moral Universalism," in Yehuda Elkana et al., eds., *Unraveling Ties—From Social Cohesion to New Practices of Connectedness* (Frankfurt and New York: Campus, 2002), 273–283.

8. As Honneth proposes; see Honneth, "A Society Without Humiliation?" 315.

9. Hans Joas, *The Genesis of Values* (Chicago: University of Chicago Press, 2000).

10. For an in-depth examination of this issue, see Joas, *Genesis of Values.*

11. Immanuel Kant, *Religion within the Limits of Reason Alone* (New York: Harper and Bros., 1960); William James, *The Will to Believe* (New York: Longmans, Green & Co., 1897); on the latter, see Joas, *Genesis of Values,* 40–43.

12. See George Herbert Mead, "The Definition of the Psychical," in *Decennial Publications of the University of Chicago,* 1st ser., vol. 3 (Chicago: University of Chicago Press, 1903), 77–112; and Mead, *Mind, Self and Society from the Standpoint of a Social Behaviorist* (Chicago: University of Chicago Press, 1934).

13. Max Scheler, "Zur Rehabilitierung der Tugend," in *Vom Umsturz der Werte,* vol. 3 of his *Gesammelte Schriften* (Bern: Francke, 1955), 13–31, esp. 17–26.

14. Joas, *Genesis of Values,* 161–186.

15. See Hans Joas, "Werte versus Normen. Das Problem der moralischen Objektivität bei Putnam, Habermas und den klassischen Pragmatisten," in Marie-Luise Raters and Marcus Willaschek, eds., *Hilary Putnam und die Tradition des Pragmatismus* (Frankfurt am Main: Suhrkamp, 2002), 263–279.

I O

Respect for Indisposability:
A Contribution to the
Bioethics Debate

The dispute over bioethical questions, and particularly about so-called therapeutic cloning, has so far distinguished itself very pleasantly from the debate on Peter Sloterdijk's provocation, in which calculated, media-savvy self-promotion and irresponsible games centered on Nietzsche's dark sides tended to divert attention away from the factual issues of bioethics. The new debate certainly features the head-on collision of differing views; it is sometimes sharp in tone. But at the same time, to a far greater extent, the protagonists are unmistakably wrestling earnestly with moral and political issues that can no longer be avoided. Perhaps all those engaged in the debate should begin by openly admitting that the new methods and potential of gene technology and the biosciences tend to unsettle their ethical certainties; and that in this new context it is far from easy to come up with a guide to action based on their ethical and religious (or antireligious) traditions. I for one certainly feel unsettled. Merely acquiring the expert biological and medical knowledge needed to discuss these issues is no mean feat. And nothing, in my opinion, helps devalue philosophical ethics more than the misplaced self-assurance of philosophers and others who have failed to examine the empirical issues in sufficient depth. As we shall see, there is also a constant danger that other debates and obsolete battles will eclipse the discussion needed now, limiting its potential to produce useful results.

As is well known, the new debate kicked off with comments by the philosopher and German government minister Julian Nida-Rümelin, which can, at the very least, be described as careless.[1] It is not his conscious attempt to set in motion a major bioethical debate in Germany and, partly as a consequence of the resolutions in the British Parliament, to discuss the pros and cons of allowing "therapeutic cloning" that deserves to be called careless. His core justificatory argument, however, is very careless indeed: "Respect for human dignity is appropriate on condition that a human being is degraded or that he or she may be robbed of self-respect. The criterion of human dignity cannot therefore be extended to embryos. The self-respect of a human embryo is not amenable to impairment." It is, of course, true that, taken as a whole, Nida-Rümelin's comments should by no means be read as a call for removing all restrictions on "therapeutic" cloning or even cloning itself; and it is thus understandable that he feels misunderstood when this political message is imputed to him. But it does nothing for the precise use of the value-laden term *human dignity* if its field of application is conceived so narrowly that it fails to tally with the pre-philosophical intuitions of contemporaries and the value traditions that nourish them. *Infancy, senility, debility*—these are just three key words indicating what respect for human dignity largely involves, and all three evade Nida-Rümelin's narrow reasoning. Its very narrowness leaves too large an area exposed to perspectives unregulated by the ideal of human dignity.

For me, it is clearly Nida-Rümelin's reasoning rather than his conclusion that Robert Spaemann is justified in calling "disgraceful."[2] Such a narrowly conceived concept of human dignity would, moreover, as I understand it, correspond neither to the understanding that applies within the German constitution nor that of any constitution under whose jurisdiction I would want to live. Spaemann is also right to expose the euphemistic nature of the term *therapeutic cloning,* the way it conceals the "use" of embryos for other purposes that are only potentially, and in a very indirect sense, therapeutic. Spaemann defends "biological belonging to the human family" as the only acceptable criterion for determining which group of people "human dignity" refers to. He thus entirely avoids discussion of the narrower question of when in the development of the human being personhood begins. He certainly leaves no doubt that for him, in terms not only of theology but also natural science, it begins with the fertilization of the egg; but he is very aware that people have sometimes had other views, even within the history of Christianity, and that to this day even those who anchor their ideas in Christian thought see things in contrasting ways. Spaemann is far from implying that the British Parliament has authorized killing. He does not really go into the empirical side of the question of whether the moment of "nidation" as legally determined in Great Britain, that is, when the fertilized egg is implanted in the womb, is an ethically acceptable criterion of personhood. But it is possible, and in my opinion vital, to distinguish the fundamental debate on the concept of human dignity from the debate, also empirical and pragmatic in nature, on when personhood begins. When people come to differing conclusions on this issue, this is quite obviously a legitimate aspect of the spectrum of opinion found in Western democracies.

The debate really began to heat up with Reinhard Merkel's contribution.[3] What appeared in the case of Nida-Rümelin, possibly counter to his intentions, as merely *permissible*, Merkel treats as nothing less than *imperative*. He leads the advocacy of "therapeutic cloning" away from a morally defensive position and turns his critique of Spaemann into an excessive and furious counterattack. For him, "the legally enshrined prohibitions in the law on the protection of embryos are certainly more than the mere expression of an exaggerated and exaggerating morality. On the contrary, in terms of their consequences (if not their motives), they are themselves morally reprehensible and thus illegitimate in terms of constitutional law." It seems to me that Merkel doesn't just *limit* the "species argument," the prohibition on killing the embryo because it belongs to the biological species *homo sapiens,* he rejects it lock, stock, and barrel. For him, it is nothing but a "naturalistic fallacy," the "derivation of a norm from a fact." Going further still, he describes as a "mystery" how the biological features shared by human beings "could justify or enjoy anything like fundamental rights" in the first place.

We might regard Nida-Rümelin's narrow concept of human dignity as the result of a counterintuitive attempt to explain a concept and the failure to reflect on the conclusions to which it leads; Merkel's furious counterattacks on Spaemann, meanwhile, are downright dangerous. Merkel is unable to see that the way in which he rejects the species argument aligns him with those who have never had anything but contempt for the principle of human equality. Of course, it is not a naturalistic fallacy if a culture decides to ascribe the same dignity to all those belonging to the human species. The question at issue is our will to do so. What we are debating are the boundaries of the group to which we can apply this ascription. Warnings against naturalistic fallacies must not be twisted to the point where they compel us to define the human being in anti-universalist fashion.

It is easy to see where the rage in Merkel's remarks comes from. Merkel is thinking more of the controversies surrounding the right to abortion than those relating to "therapeutic cloning." He rekindles the battle over this right, his scorn and ridicule far more apparent than his understanding of how difficult it is to strike a balance between values and between differing conceptions of values; it is this balancing act that is responsible for the complex solution adopted in Germany. This stance seems to me to give the lie to the author's self-presentation as an Enlightenment liberal. Reviving the dead ends and divisions of the abortion debate is precisely what we have to avoid in the bioethical debate. The resentment felt toward religiously grounded ethics and its reservations about the scientifically feasible might have historic roots, but as things stand today, the idea that science has to be set free from religious and ethical "shackles" is simply misleading.

The same Enlightenment countermyth is present in the work of Christoph Türcke,[4] but is now twisted even further, in that nothing other than Christianity is declared the wellspring of the technological and scientific mania for feasibility. Here, the argument appears to rest on such shaky foundations that the association between eugenics and the name of Pope Eugene is evoked to back up the thesis that there can be "no religion without eugenics." This is not an argument worthy of refutation but rather a symptom of what seems to me the real dilemma of this debate: the eclipsing of bioethical issues by old battle lines based on such notions as "Enlightenment versus religion." Overcoming these divisions is the only way to move forward in the contemporary debate. In my view, with respect to all political issues that involve human rights and human dignity, our sole priority today must be to bring together all those who share the same values and wish to see them having a major political impact. The preamble to the Polish constitution, which states that the constitution is anchored in values that some people experience as binding for religious reasons and others for different reasons, seems to me to articulate this stance best. In Poland, the experience of totalitarianism was decisive in creating this perspective. In the present context, the old divisions are rendered obsolete by another factor. We are faced with a situation in which the sphere of the formerly indisposable is dwindling as a result of scientific progress and social changes. There was no need to make many decisions in the past, because there was simply no way of influencing certain events. But if it is possible—and necessary—to decide, perhaps to an extent with which individuals and their polities struggle to cope, then the crucial question is no longer how to gain yet more options, but whether there should be limits on disposability. Rather than interpreting every limitation as a restriction on our freedom, the key issue here is our will to draw the line and to voluntarily respect indisposability.

That, in my opinion, is what it means to speak of human dignity; the intention is to establish the absolute value of every human being, a value that is sacrosanct, independent of all individual forms the human being may take. I have criticized Merkel for failing to see the extent to which the bioethical debate revolves around our will to respect such boundaries. Human rights and human dignity do, in fact, rest upon a "will to believe" (William James). Otfried Höffe[5] is confident that he has found a watertight rational justification for this belief in Kant's philosophy. I do not share his confidence, but the question of foundationalist philosophical claims can safely be placed in parentheses here. At least for the social sciences and for politics, we are concerned not only with the *justification* of values but also their *genesis,* not only with rational arguments but also constitutive experiences. We wish to identify the historical origins of the belief in human rights and human dignity; how this belief takes shape within the development of individual personhood; and how present-day individuals can find new ways to adequately articulate a belief that certainly has deep historical roots, but that has only had a profound impact since the eighteenth century and, above all, in the second half of the twentieth century.

Although the roots of this belief in human dignity, even in its secularized forms, undoubtedly lie in the Judeo-Christian tradition, this is no reason for Christian triumphalism—Christians have certainly had their difficulties with the idea of human rights after these took palpable form in the American and French Revolutions for the first time. At times, it was necessary to wrest from the Christian churches what seems to us today a taken-for-granted expression of the spirit of the Gospels. Charles Taylor argues that under certain conditions the (Enlightenment) break with Christianity was a necessary condition for the further development of Christian values.[6] At a time when people are rightly searching for the genuine potential, in all cultural traditions, for the belief in human rights and human dignity, this productive curiosity must again be directed with increased vigor at our own—Christian—tradition, which has largely been forgotten or is registered only in stereotypical form.

Much effort is, no doubt, needed to articulate this in new ways. If personhood is understood through the concept of the soul in the Christian tradition, the disappearance of a notion of the soul rooted in the metaphysics of substance must not, for example, cause us to throw the baby out with the bathwater and pass up the opportunity to formulate in new ways the meaningful content of the concept of the soul. If the Judeo-Christian tradition has interpreted the life of the human being as a gift, then this, too, opens up a perspective that should not be ignored by those who do not believe that this gift is bestowed by a transcendent being. One of the greatest postwar sociologists, Talcott Parsons, devoted much of his later work to the task of reformulating this idea in a way appropriate to the contemporary era. The origins of the idea of human dignity lie not only in contexts of Enlightenment but also in religiously motivated struggles over freedom of religion—for one's own faith but also that of others. And the shock felt at the "debasement" of the human being, the traumas of the twentieth century, have played a significant role in intensifying and disseminating our belief in human dignity.

All these remarks are simply pointers intended to help counter the eclipse of the bioethical debate in Germany by another debate altogether. If it is true, as the great French sociologist Émile Durkheim claimed toward the end of the nineteenth century, that the belief in human rights and human dignity is the "religion" capable of achieving consensus in a modern, individualized world,[7] then rather than wasting our energies fighting old battles, we ought to pool them in a common effort to defend human dignity—in a context in which we are compelled to make decisions on an ever-expanding range of subjects and in which very little in the realms of nature and tradition can be taken for granted.

One often encounters the fallacy that increasing freedom of choice is itself a reason for the dramatic decline in, or impossibility of, long-term commitment—whether with respect to people, communities, or values. But commitment has other sources, which are generally more significant than the merely rational knowledge of the diverse range of alternatives. The profoundly affective attachment to the value of "human dignity" has only just begun to gain momentum within our culture. Against all the claims of declining values, it is striking how profoundly the human dignity of, for example, children or women or nonwhite peoples has inspired real changes, often only in the recent past. There is no sensible reason to inhibit this momentum. It cannot be halted, even if it has consequences for the human dignity of the unborn child with which liberal individualism might not have initially reckoned.

As long as it appeared that the self-determination of the individual was the leading value of modern societies, it was indeed possible to respond to the ethical problems of abortion with the slogan "it's my belly," epitomizing the refusal to acknowledge that this issue at least entails colliding values. But the more the notion of "human dignity" gains momentum, the clearer it is becoming that it does not mean giving free reign to individualism but respecting the other's indisposability. And this other might be an embryo.

And what does this mean for "therapeutic cloning"? Our respect for the indisposability of the other must be our ethical guide; but this does not allow us to deduce when the personhood begins. In this sense, I can see room for maneuver between Spaemann's insistence on the moment of fertilization and the British regulations, which refer to the implantation of the egg in the womb fourteen days after fertilization. But the meta-rule must certainly be based on maximum caution. Only when all other possibilities have truly been exhausted and clear evidence exists that worthy aims cannot be achieved in any other way, should cloning be permitted. And it seems to me that we lack such evidence as yet.

NOTES

1. Julian Nida-Rümelin, "Wo die Menschenwürde beginnt," *Der Tagesspiegel,* January 3, 2001. See the following compilations of contributions to the debate: *Die Zeit,* Dokument 1 (2002); Christian Geyer, ed., *Biopolitik* (Frankfurt am Main: Suhrkamp, 2001).

2. Robert Spaemann, "Gezeugt, nicht gemacht," *Die Zeit,* January 18, 2001.

3. Reinhard Merkel, "Rechte für Embryonen," *Die Zeit,* January 25, 2001.

4. Christoph Türcke, "Der schmale Grat der Demut," *Die Zeit,* February 8, 2001.

5. Otfried Höffe, "Wessen Menschenwürde," *Die Zeit,* February 1, 2001.

6. See the chapter on Taylor, "A Catholic Modernity?" in this volume.

7. See the final chapter of this volume, "Human Dignity: The Religion of Modernity?"

I I

Human Dignity:
The Religion of Modernity?

I would like to develop my argument with reference to a key event in the intellectual and political history of Europe, which occurred in the last few years of the nineteenth century. The year was 1898, the location France. This year saw the birth of both the French Human Rights League and the ultranationalist, proto-fascist, and anti-Semitic Action Française. Both movements were outcomes of the same conflict, which rocked the country and almost split it into two camps—the so-called Affaire Dreyfus. Let me briefly remind you of the facts. In December 1894, the Jewish-Alsatian artillery captain and general staff officer Alfred Dreyfus was accused of high treason, that is, of passing defense secrets to Germany, dishonorably discharged from the French army, and sentenced to lifelong deportation to Devil's Island. In the years after his conviction, more and more doubts arose regarding the evidence adduced against him and the rightfulness of the court's decision. In 1897, the judgment was appealed against, and from then on (but particularly after the sensational open letter by Émile Zola addressed to the president of the republic, published January 13, 1898, with its blaring headline "J'accuse") what had been a matter for the judiciary turned into a political affair of the highest order. On February 20, 1898, the Human Rights League was founded. Initially, its sole aim was to achieve a retrial and prevent the "honor of the army" or latent anti-Semitism from tipping the balance against the probably innocent captain. In early September 1898, the chain of events reached its dramatic climax when it emerged that the director of the military secret service had been arrested in late August and confessed to having falsified a decisive document incriminating Dreyfus. A day after his confession, he took his own life in jail. After this sensation, Dreyfus's conviction was, of course, no longer tenable. It was at first annulled, then commuted to a mere prison sentence, for which Dreyfus received an amnesty enabling his immediate release. It was only years later, in 1906, that Dreyfus was finally acquitted, but in such a way that some remained unconvinced of his innocence despite all the evidence.

The enormous emotion and polarization triggered by these events have been documented in innumerable writings, including great literature, ranging from Marcel Proust to Roger Martin du Gard. In her book on totalitarianism, Hannah Arendt claimed that late nineteenth-century France prefigured the political cleavages of the twentieth century in much the same way as the French Revolution foreshadowed nineteenth century history.[1] This certainly applies to the Dreyfus affair. It also applies to the spread and the intellectual penetration of the belief in human rights and to the radical rejection of this belief.

The most intellectually consistent argument produced thus far as to why we should regard belief in human rights and universal human dignity as the "religion of modernity" resulted from this conflict. The author of this text was the greatest French sociologist, one of the classical figures of the nascent discipline, Émile Durkheim. He was a founding member of the Human Rights League and secretary of its Bordeaux chapter.[2] Articles such as Charles Maurras's "The first blood,"[3] which agitated for struggle against the Dreyfusards even if Dreyfus should be innocent, resulted from the same context. For Maurras, the rights of the individual or human dignity are minor concerns when an institution such as the army or the well-being of the nation is at stake. A violation of these rights, even a lie or falsification, is then justified in a higher sense—or, rather, requires no justification. Just as Mussolini later encouraged his fascist militias to engage in violence without even maintaining the facade of instrumental or moral justification, this entails crossing a line, one that twentieth-century fascist movements were to scornfully and systematically ignore. It is important to underline the twofold character of the intellectual reactions to the Dreyfus conflict, because awareness of this ambiguity helps guard against the drawing of unfounded optimistic conclusions on the basis of certain affinities between the structures of modern societies and the belief in human dignity, affinities to which I shall now turn.

Durkheim kicks off his argument, which is intended to demonstrate the "sacredness" of the individual in modernity, by highlighting the profound ambiguity of the term *individualism*. He considers this a pressing matter because the so-called Anti-Dreyfusards accused all those willing to accept the weakening of the army's authority and who "obstinately refuse to bend their logic before the word of an army general"[4] of promoting "individualism" (43). On this view, such individualism would mean the end of all social order and sense of commonality; it was the "great sickness of the present age." Durkheim concedes that such a destructive, anarchic individualism does indeed exist. According to him, it can be found whenever individuals lack a higher goal than maximization of egotistical pleasure or economic utility. He yields to no one in his criticism of such individualism. But he regards it as completely unacceptable to identify this type of individualism in any way with the moral philosophy of Kant or Rousseau or the individualism "which the Declaration of the Rights of Man attempted, more or less happily, to formulate" (45).

Such sentiments suggest that this second type of individualism is more or less the opposite of the egotistical variety; interests of a merely personal nature are viewed with skepticism or, as in Kant, almost as the source of evil. Such individualism has nothing in common with "that apotheosis of well-being and private interest" and "that egoistic cult of the self for which utilitarian individualism has been rightly criticized" (45).

Individualists of this second type, far from abandoning themselves to the impulses arising from their pre-given nature, gear themselves toward an ambitious ideal, that of acting in a way of which all human beings might in principle approve or, to put it philosophically, such that the maxim underlying their action is amenable to universalization. Durkheim writes:

> This ideal so far surpasses the level of utilitarian goals that it seems to those minds who aspire to it to be completely stamped with religiosity. This human person (*personne humaine*), the definition of which is like the touchstone which distinguishes good from evil, is considered sacred in the ritual sense of the word. It partakes of the transcendent majesty that churches of all time lend to their gods;

it is conceived of as being invested with that mysterious property which creates a void about sacred things, which removes them from vulgar contacts and withdraws them from common circulation. And the respect which is given it comes precisely from this source. Whoever makes an attempt on a man's life, on a man's liberty, on a man's honor, inspires in us a feeling of horror analogous in every way to that which the believer experiences when he sees his idol profaned. Such an ethic is therefore not simply a hygienic discipline or a prudent economy of existence; it is a religion in which man is at once the worshiper and the god. (45)

Following this long quotation, we should pause for a moment for the sake of conceptual clarification. I find the distinction between two types of individualism convincing, although one would have to pin down more precisely what constitutes purely egotistical individualism. Even the utilitarian paradigm that Durkheim clearly had in mind here cannot be dismissed as readily as he implied. Moreover, we would have to add a third version of individualism that goes beyond the Kantian moralistic version, a Herderian variety for which not moral duty but self-realization is the guiding value. This expressivist-romantic alternative does not occur to Durkheim at all.[5] But his own distinction between types of individualism is certainly important even today and is an advance on his own earlier attacks on the destructive effects of individualism.

Furthermore, Durkheim speaks of the "sacrality" or "sacredness" of the person. He does not refer to Kant here, although he could have done so, because Kant speaks of sacredness at precisely the point where he introduces the concept of *dignity* (in his *Grundlegung zur Metaphysik der Sitten*). For Kant, dignity is that which is and must be priceless; it is "exalted above all price and so admits of no equivalent."[6] It is impossible to compare the mode of thought characteristic of the concept of dignity with that relating to the prices of goods "without, as it were, violating its holiness."[7]

But that which is a mere momentary conceptual intuition in Kant's work is for Durkheim the point of departure for his developing theory of religion and for the idea that the person himself has become the sacred object of modern societies. I will return to this point shortly.

Two additional conceptual clarifications are necessary. Durkheim speaks alternately of the sacredness of the individual and of the person, as if these two concepts were interchangeable. If there is no risk of the concept of the individual being misunderstood along utilitarian and egotistical lines, this is unproblematic. Durkheim can then interpret the cult of the individual for the sake of the individual as a superstitious and decadent form of authentic individualism. I refer to the sacredness of the *person* rather than that of the *individual* to make completely sure that the belief in the irreducible dignity of all human beings is not conflated with an egocentric self-sacralization of the individual, a narcissist inability to transcend one's self-centeredness.

Durkheim thus articulates the belief in human rights and human dignity as the expression of a process of the sacralization of the person. In this sense, his ascription to the person of the same aura characteristic of all sacred objects is understandable and apt. But Durkheim characteristically overstates his case when he calls the morality of human rights a religion "in which man is at once the worshiper and the god." By demonstrating the fruitfulness of his idea of the sacredness of the person, he has by no means shown that human beings are the source of their own sacralization. Durkheim, the rabbi's son, allows his programmatic atheism to distort his argument here. If we take this lacuna in his argument to be symptomatic, we can say that his atheism was dogmatic. Durkheim fails to open himself to the possibility that belief in the sacredness of the person can have competing origins; he is closed to the idea that religion might in the future support human rights. This will become even clearer in what follows.

Durkheim's next step is an attempt to demonstrate that such a belief, which he calls, following Auguste Comte, "la religion de l'humanité," the religion of mankind or humanity, is assuredly capable of integrating whole societies. In his book on the division of labor, he had still defended a different assumption, namely, that "the cult of the individual" is an anomaly among beliefs and values, because it directs the will toward a common goal that is not social and thus cannot contribute to the formation of authentic social bonds.[8] Durkheim has now overcome his earlier skepticism: He has recognized the difference between glorification of one's own ego and the sacralization of the human person as such. "It springs not from egoism but from sympathy for all that is human, a broader pity for all sufferings, for all human miseries, a more ardent need to combat them and mitigate them, a greater thirst for justice" (48f.) Durkheim then briefly rejects the possible objection that freedom of opinion leads to anarchy by demonstrating how scientific discourse, given absolute freedom of thought, is fully capable of generating consensus and rational authority. He then goes one decisive step further. For him, the sacredness of the person is not just *one* possible belief system with socially integrative effects but the only system of beliefs that can "ensure the moral unity of the country" in the future. This far-reaching claim imposes on Durkheim a dual burden of proof. On the one hand, he must show that modern societies have certain structural features that make it functionally necessary to generate social integration by means of moral individualism. On the other hand, he must delineate the relationship between this moral individualism and traditional religions. His contribution to the Dreyfus debate, of course, fails to cover either point in real depth.

Nonetheless, his basic line of argument is fairly clear, and it is to this that we must now turn. There can be no doubt that Durkheim, the alleged functionalist, has no time for those who champion the strengthening of religion in order to increase social harmony. And it is indeed true that nobody can become a religious believer just because it would be socially advantageous were she to do so.[9] Although it is a sociological truism that "a society cannot be coherent if there does not exist among its members a certain intellectual and moral community" (51), pleas for community do little to bring it about. Moreover, it might be that in new circumstances old forms of community are no longer viable so that pleas for a return to old forms of social integration frequently involve the articulation of a problem rather than a solution. For Durkheim, the only solution is the sacralization of the person, because it is the only way of reconstituting the social bond that avoids flying in the face of the very structural tendencies that made maintenance of the traditional bonds impossible. Two such structural tendencies are mentioned: the territorial expansion of societies and the advancing division of labor. The larger a society is in a spatial sense, the more difficult it is, according to Durkheim, to achieve uniformity of traditions and practices. One might add that this remains irrelevant as long as there is no interaction between the inhabitants of different parts of a country. But as soon as this interaction, and commerce, increases, differences must be tolerated or systematically repressed. If they are tolerated, there will be many variants rather than one unitary culture. The increasing division of labor reinforces this tendency even in small regions. Professional specialization, for example, gives rise to different skills, competencies, attitudes, and perspectives. Division of labor and territorial expansion thus lead to a state of affairs in which people are less and less able to identify with one another on the basis of particular features they have in common. The only source of a shared culture is then "this idea of the human person ... the only idea which would be retained, unalterable and impersonal, above the changing torrent of individual opinions" (51f.).

And what is the relationship between this idea and the Christian faith? Durkheim assumes that this conception of the human person is a contemporary articulation of the impulses that originally brought Christianity into being:

> Whereas the religion of the ancient city-state was quite entirely made of external practices, from which the spiritual was absent, Christianity demonstrated in its inner faith, in the personal conviction of the individual, the essential condition of piety. First, it taught that the moral value of acts had to be measured according to the intention, a preeminently inward thing which by its very nature escapes all external judgments and which only the agent could competently appraise. The very center of moral life was thus transported from the external to the internal, and the individual was thus elevated to be sovereign judge of his own conduct, accountable only to himself and to his God. (52)

Christianity's importance to the cultural prerequisites for the emergence of modern individualism thus cannot be exaggerated. Durkheim took a great interest in these cultural processes, with regard, for example, to the concept of the *soul* in Christianity and its continuity with ideas found in primitive religions,[10] the role of Christianity in the history of education in the occident, and legal history. In his political-moral declaration of 1898, he consequently rejects any assumption that he favors breaking with the Christian tradition. On the contrary, he presents his plea for human rights as a continuation of that tradition. But for him, to continue a tradition is to overcome it. From this viewpoint, Christianity is a form of "restrained individualism" and now has to be replaced by "a more fully developed individualism" (53). The belief in human rights is thus not embedded in Christianity; it is to take the place of that religion, which is claimed merely to have laid the ground for this modern faith.

Sociology after Durkheim has produced a wealth of studies and reflections on the potential functions of a belief in human rights and human dignity under modern conditions and on the expression of this belief in everyday social interaction. In the main, Durkheim emphasized the division of labor or functional differentiation between actors and societal subsystems as the main feature of modern societies. His reference to territorial scope played only a secondary role, because he generally considered size and density prerequisites for setting in motion processes of differentiation. The sociological literature after Durkheim goes further than he did in emphasizing the importance of cultural pluralism in general—a pluralism that is not necessarily the result of functional differentiation, but that might also come about in other ways, for example, through migration, value change, and cultural diffusion. But there is no doubt that functional differentiation increases the need for integrative resources—what Talcott Parsons called "societal community," an expression that must sound paradoxical if one assumes that there is a dichotomous distinction between "community" and "society." In our time, Niklas Luhmann (in his book *The Law of Society*) has radicalized Durkheim's approach. For Luhmann, a strict causal connection exists between increasing functional differentiation and the codification of subjective rights; the former leads to the growing autonomy of the individual subsystems and increasingly reduces human beings to mere elements of the environment of systems rather than assuming that they are constitutive of them. The individual, according to Luhmann, is compensated for the loss of all fixed social positions by gaining subjective rights:[11] The legal system becomes a system of compensation for the consequences faced by the individual when society is restructured in such a way that functional differentiation increases. For Luhmann, this functional relationship makes it entirely predictable and plausible that human rights would be codified for the first time during a period when functional differentiation was advancing with particular vigor, namely, during what is called the *Sattelzeit* around 1800. For Luhmann, it also stands to reason that today at a time of so-called globalization—another step forward in the global division of labor—the institutionalization of human rights is also advancing.

But one might object that such a bird's-eye perspective completely fails to bring out the concrete historical processes that led to the emergence and dissemination of human rights. The alleged functional relationships, as plausible as they might be, were certainly not evident to the historical actors. It would be terribly reductionist, therefore, to assume that questions like that of whether human rights spring from religious or nonreligious roots can thus be declared settled or irrelevant. Durkheim himself paved the way for an addi-tional and alternative view. The individualism he was talking about was—in his eyes—not so much a philosophical system but one of a "practical and not theoretical nature. If individualism is to be what it is, it must penetrate the mores and the organs of society."[12] Like every religion, the religion of humanity should be judged not by its dogmas but by its practices, its rituals. In two areas, Durkheim himself undertook pioneering efforts to apply these insights. First, he had a strong interest in how the role of punitive justice had changed on the way to modernity.[13] Killing, which we moderns take to be the most abominable of crimes, particularly if it is arbitrary or cruel, was not always thought of in this way. In premodern societies, whose sacred core does not revolve around the human person, this evaluation is absent. There, the worst crimes are violations of the transcendent or mundane incarnation of the sacred, such as blasphemy, sacrilege, or regicide. It is not only the evaluation of actions that changes dramatically within the framework of these processes but also ideas about punishment. Torture as a means of producing confessions or as punishment in public is increasingly experienced as incompatible with the dignity of man, including criminals. The whole system of punitive justice changes, becoming more oriented toward imprison-ment or resocialization; it undergoes a process of humanization. This is a far from simple or linear process. One need only think of the persistence of "lynching" in the racist milieu of the U.S. South well into the twentieth century. Opinions on whether the death penalty as such is cruel or only certain forms of execution are, differ markedly not only between Europeans and Americans, but also among Americans. Many contemporary readers learn about this process from Michel Foucault's famous book *Discipline and Punish*, which uncovers the downside of modern forms of punitive justice in impressive fashion, but in a way that practically negates the civilizational progress that this process nonetheless entails.[14]

The other field of research to which Durkheim himself contrib-uted in this regard is concerned with the changing culture of rational argumentation. Science, for him, is one aspect of the development of moral individualism—not the most fundamental aspect, but an important one. Science, too, is based on a belief in the essential worth of each individual. "The 'dogma' of this faith is the autonomy of reason, its 'rite' to verify all claims to validity" (49). The American pragmatists developed this insight even further, concluding that since no one can predict where cognitive innovation might arise, the social status of the speaker is irrelevant; each proposition must be examined according to the validity of its truth claims.

Durkheim's own research methods, however, focused on the *institutions* of law and science rather than on their *practice*. He did not deal microscopically with topics such as the legal knowledge of actors, the structures of legal discourse, or the dynamics of scientific argumentation. Since Durkheim, both sociology and history have moved in this direction. This microscopic analysis is particularly important when dealing with the sacralization of the person in everyday life, in rules of greeting, interaction rituals, mutual face-saving in conflicts, politeness, and so on. Erving Goffman's writings can be read as Machiavellian guidebooks for strategic impression management, but also as studies of the sacralization of the person in everyday life.[15] An abundance of other examples exists. The interaction between doctors and patients is changing, as the latter increasingly demand respect. One generation ago, medical paternalism allowed or even recommended keeping patients in the dark about certain diagnoses (as in the case of cancer) or therapies. Today, surgery without the informed consent of the patient is considered a crime. Increased public awareness of sexual harassment, child pornography, or sexual abuse of children by pedophile priests is not the result of an increase in these offenses but of increasing sensitivity to the destructive character of such acts. All public discourse on loss of values must be balanced by taking into account these examples of increasing moral sensitization.

The connection I have in mind between the sacralization of the person and intense experiences can be illustrated by turning to the field of sexuality. In an almost unknown text, namely, the summary of a debate in Paris in 1911 on problems of sexual education, we can detect Durkheim's position on this matter.[16] He found himself confronted by medical doctors for whom sexuality was nothing but a bodily process and who propagated the radical dismantling of what they saw as a web of prejudices, norms, and fantasies surrounding this process. Although Durkheim was firmly in favor of sexual education, he was against such a reductionist conception of sexuality. As a sociologist, he could not disregard the fact that in all cultures sexuality has an aura of the "mysterious"; a truly rational interpretation, he thought, should never consider such an aura a mere prejudice. Sexuality, he states, has a double character, being anti-moral and constitutive of morality at one and the same time. I am aware of the risk of being misunderstood here. Reference to the anti-moral character of sexuality sounds like prudishness today. But if we accept—against Norbert Elias—the finding of cultural anthropologists that shame is culturally universal and sexual activity does not take place in public even in cultures in which nakedness is the norm, then Durkheim is right to describe the transgression of the boundaries of shame as one of the features of sexuality. Insofar as shame is not only an empirically verifiable psychological phenomenon but also a virtue in all cultures, though certainly not to the same extent, we might state that sexuality always negates this virtue to some degree. But as I have said, sexuality is also constitutive of morality; the sexual act, in Durkheim's own words, is "foncièrement moralisateur,"[17] "profoundly constitutive of morality." This might sound even stranger today than the notion of the amoral character of sexuality. Sexual experience is constitutive of morality, because it is one of the most important sources of deep-seated affective ties among human beings. A merely biological perspective fails to do justice to the way in which shared sexual experience generates social bonds, distorting the specifically human character of sexuality. All cultures therefore fence in sexuality with specific institutions and ideas. In an age of increasing sacralization of the person, this "fencing in" is growing in importance. This might sound implausible, given all the talk of sexual liberalization today. But the term *liberalization* fails to capture the increasing sensitivity to sexual abuse and harassment referred to previously. If we take seriously the parallel between the aura of sacred objects and the aura of the person under the condition of sacralization, we can see why physically approaching another person without following certain prescribed rules is experienced as profanation. Respect for the sacredness of the person entails respect for the free will of the other. Physical distance is an expression of such respect, and sexuality tends to abolish this distance. It might lead to the experience of communion, a fusion with another person that negates, for an ecstatic moment, the boundaries separating our identities. This is the experience of self-transcendence that gives rise to attachment to others as well as to values. It is not surprising then that sexual relations change under the influence of the sacralization of the person.

   This example leads on to the complex question of how the different levels of the sacralization of the person interconnect. When Durkheim speaks of the belief in human dignity as the "religion" of modernity, he is thinking of a belief system but also its manifestation in law and other institutions and in everyday practices of public and intimate interaction. But it is far from clear that he successfully analyzes the interconnection of these levels and identifies the historical and existential foundations of the ideal of moral individualism. There is much disagreement over whether the notion of the "religion" of modernity is appropriate in the first place. It is true that human dignity is not simply a moral and normative imperative but an ideal with an intense affective charge. But this "religion" lacks a cult in the sense of special rituals or a genuine church, a community of the faithful. This is not because this individualist ideal has no need of such practical and institutional supports. Durkheim himself had no real answer to the question of which institutions might undergird it. He was forced to tackle this question precisely because his original progressive optimism gradually came to seem implausible. His study of the elementary forms of religious life, primarily totemism, was clearly motivated by these questions. But in a sense he never really returned from his imaginary research trips among the Australian Aborigines and North American Indians. He ascribes to the democratic state and professional associations, revitalized on the model of the guilds, a key role in embodying and maintaining this ideal. But this cannot be the last word on this, not only because his political objectives with respect to professional groups remained ridden with aporiae, but because his solution was overly abstract. We need to grapple far more concretely with existing religious and national traditions and historical experiences, if we wish to do justice to the interplay among state, civil society, and values in the history of human rights.

With regard to national traditions, Durkheim focused on the case of France. He saw a continuity between the principles of 1789 and the struggle for human rights in France in his own time:

> And if there is a country among all others, where the cause of individualism is truly national, it is our own; for there is no other which has created such rigorous solidarity between its fate and the fate of these ideas. We have given them their most recent formulation, and it is from us that other peoples have received them. And this is why even now we are considered their most authoritative representatives. Therefore we cannot disavow them today without disavowing ourselves, without diminishing ourselves in the eyes of the world, without committing a veritable moral suicide. (54)

As impressive as this plea might have sounded in France, the fusion of universalism and French nationalism can only be perceived skeptically beyond its borders. U.S. missionary universalism is a parallel phenomenon; in both cases, national interests are frequently couched in universalist terms. But in both countries, there are indeed public rituals, symbols, myths, and institutions that support moral individualism in the Durkheimian sense.

Durkheim's ideas with respect to religious traditions were far less compelling. He was right to claim that such traditions must be continued in creative ways; that new forms of moral individualism exert a certain pressure on them to express and articulate themselves anew. We tend to think of Islam in this respect today, but we should not forget how difficult it was for Catholicism and much of European Protestantism as well to develop a positive relationship to human rights, religious freedom, democracy, market economics, and world peace. From 1791 on, the official doctrine of the Catholic Church assailed human rights, because they were perceived as an aspect of the anticlerical and antireligious heritage of the French Revolution; the church supported the anti-Dreyfusards in the Dreyfus affair. This changed only in the mid-twentieth century. Durkheim's attempt to describe Christianity as an obsolete forerunner of the secular religion of modernity is, in my view, the flipside of an anti-modernist self-understanding of the church.

But we do not have to choose between these two options. It is possible for religion to be individualized if the churches accept individuals' increasing demand for moral self-determination and self-realization. The spirit of the Gospel could thus support the struggle for human rights. This is a necessary development, because this struggle is not over. My emphasis on the complex interplay of values, institutions, and practices is intended to underline that the realization of these ideals is never guaranteed. Durkheim's historical optimism is untenable if we take the experiences of the twentieth century seriously. For him, the structure of modern societies makes the institutionalization of human rights inevitable. "For in order to halt its advance it would be necessary ... to contain ... the tendency for societies to become always more extended and more centralized, and to place an obstacle in the way of the unceasing progress of the division of labor. Such an enterprise, whether desirable or not, infinitely exceeds all human capability" (52). After the twentieth century, we have to make clear that Durkheim was too optimistic in this respect.

The proto-fascist Action Française might have shown little creativity and enjoyed little success, but Italian fascism and German Nazism were not simply anti-modernist. They were attempts to develop alternative modernities without the values articulated in the human rights catalogues. We do not know whether the twenty-first century will see new attempts of this kind. This is why the institutionalization of human rights remains dependent on the active support of each new generation.

NOTES

1. Hannah Arendt, *The Origins of Totalitarianism* (London: Deutsch, 1986; originally published in 1951), 79.

2. Steven Lukes, *Émile Durkheim: His Life and Work* (Harmondsworth, England: Penguin, 1977), 347–349.

3. See Ernst Nolte, *Der Faschismus in seiner Epoche* (Munich: Piper, 1984), 92.

4. Émile Durkheim, "Individualism and the Intellectuals" (1898), in Robert N. Bellah, ed., *Émile Durkheim on Morality and Society* (Chicago: University of Chicago Press, 1986), 43–57, esp. 43; subsequent page references in the text refer to this essay.

5. See Hans Joas, *The Creativity of Action* (Chicago: University of Chicago Press, 1992).

6. Immanuel Kant, *Groundwork for the Metaphysics of Morals* (Oxford: Oxford University Press, 2002; originally published in 1785), 235.

7. Ibid., 236.

8. Émile Durkheim, *The Division of Labor in Society* (New York: Free Press, 1997; originally published in 1893), 201f.

9. For a more detailed examination of this issue, see the opening chapter of this volume.

10. Émile Durkheim, *The Elementary Forms of Religious Life* (Oxford: Oxford University Press, 2001; originally published in 1912), 242–275; Durkheim, *The Evolution of Educational Thought* (London: Routledge, 1977; originally published in 1938); Durkheim, *Professional Ethics and Civic Morals* (London: Routledge, 1991).

11. Niklas Luhmann, *Das Recht der Gesellschaft* (Frankfurt am Main: Suhrkamp, 1993), 487.

12. Durkheim, *Professional Ethics,* 88.

13. Émile Durkheim, "Deux lois de l'évolution pénale," in *Journal sociologique* (Paris: Presses Universitaires des France, 1969; originally published in 1901), 244–273.

14. Michel Foucault, *Discipline and Punish: The Birth of the Prison* (New York: Vintage, 1977).

15. Randall Collins in particular has persistently championed such an interpretation.

16. Émile Durkheim, "Débat sur l'éducation sexuelle," in *Textes,* vol. 2 (Paris: Éditions de Minuit, 1975; originally published in 1911), 241–251.

17. Ibid., 248.

Index

About the Author

Hans Joas, born 1948 in Munich (Germany), is the director of the Max Weber Center for Advanced Cultural and Social Studies in Erfurt (Germany) and professor of sociology at the University of Chicago, where he also belongs to the Committee on Social Thought. His most recent publications in English are *The Genesis of Values* (University of Chicago Press, 2000), *War and Modernity* (Blackwell, 2003), *Social Theory* (with W. Knoebl) (in German 2004, English translation: Cambridge University Press, 2008).